Reality and Shit
By Fritz Blackburn
Copyright © 2016 Fritz Blackburn

No part of this book may be reproduced in any form or by any electronic or mechanical means including information storage and retrieval systems, without permission in writing from the author. The only exception is by a reviewer, who may quote short excerpts in a review.

Online copy provided in New Zealand

Contents - Index

Introduction

Introduction

We have all heard the sound of battle, standing outside a row of toilets, with thick, deadly smells squeezing through the gaps around the door, invading our nostrils and lungs with the most intimate, if undesired, knowledge of the inner person on the other side of the dividing door...

We have listened to their groans and sighs, squeezed with them in sympathy for their ordeal, hoping they will succeed eventually, so we too may get a chance to do our own thing, our very own way, soon.

One does, in such meditations, form a spontaneous picture of the person who might be grunting and bubbling there, one meter away from us, after attending his life-struggles for a full ten minutes! It is not like we imagine a big fat customer working away in there and then the door opens and a skinny weasel runs out of the toilet! Things are not like that. Things are connected!

A big fat job on the toilet goes with certain kinds of grunting, certain efforts and particular smells, that all go together. There is a harmony in the world that allows you to *see* a person pretty accurately if you but listen and smell them for a bit.

The door opens—and the guy that comes out is just the guy you visualized! Sometimes it is then difficult not to smile at him like at an old acquaintance. But people don't like it much when you look at them as if you knew them, when they've just come through that door...

So yes, we have all suffered these experiences, even if we never made comment, always kept our facial muscles pleasant, the lips only slightly puckered and the traitorous nose well controlled.

People get away with anything they do in toilets uncensored because nobody will ever look or speak of it to them...It is our greatest taboo! Only the very assertive would wrinkle their noses at employees and colleagues or at the boss's wife.

I think it is essential to look at truth and reality as they actually are, by facing up even to those supposed darker aspects of our lives that we have been told not to bring up in sophisticated conversation and therefore never learn from or include into our world view.

"Looking at your shit" is a modern psychological term for owning one's actions and burdens from the past(karma) and for taking responsibility. Literally to look at your shit, especially when it includes the sense of smell, has just that same psychological effect and is in my experience more effective in achieving self-knowledge than psychology or spiritual workshops. I've tried it! I've smelled it all, seen it, and happily live to talk about it!

So, shall we dare examine some fundamental human questions, like—what has a real foul smell got to do with our diet? And with our emotions? Or—what is really a "bad" smell?

Why is our language so full of "shit?" Why does dieting not work? How can we lose weight and keep it off? What is fundamentally wrong with our "economy?"

The way we poop tells a whole lot about who we really are and it symbolizes all other aspects of our lives, including how we have sex, how we dream, eat and work.

Also, the way we avoid talking about the *other side* of eating, tells a lot about how we divide reality into what we find acceptable and what we choose to ignore. We never see the whole picture!

Even doctors and teachers avoid the subject entirely or replace commonly understood terms with "scientific" and sterile words that contain no smells and mystify clear understanding.

It has always annoyed me shitless that even in otherwise good books, the heroes never need to go behind the bush! They are chained to dungeon walls for days, or bundled into rescue boats, or dressed as the opposite sex, but they never seem to take a dump? How do they do that?

Movies are worse—you see Arnie and Sly in full battle gear, fighting it out for days uninterrupted, but they never go for so much as a piss! Is that possible?

Pretty ladies poop even less and use the "bathroom" only to "powder their noses," apply make-up or talk to their sisters...

Shit is one of our greatest taboos, which causes a myriad of illnesses, poor sex and failure of all diets, a lack of self-knowledge, economic loss and not so body-wise literature.

On the other hand, human excrement is the most undervalued commodity in all of western society! Only bull-shit is valued much more highly...

We need to realize that shitting is as important as eating, as natural as breathing, and that our taboo is in no way sensible, reasonable, or even affordable.

To focus on the ignored, on the dark and un-discussed issues of our time can have much more actual value for the spiritual seeker than to chant mantras or to attend yoga-classes! To deal with one's shit is a "yoga of the simple person" who has neither time nor money for self-development workshops and prefers a solidly grounded spiritual discipline that has no masters, no gurus, no industry and no bull attached to it. It is a path of truth that overcomes division and reveals oneness!

Conscious shitting offers precisely what solid spiritual practise should be: common, not far-fetched; truly honest, not above the clouds; smelly, not sterile; intense, yet authentic.

To talk about shit is itself a therapy that restores one of the greatest imbalances in our awareness and offers solutions on a physical, emotional, mental and spiritual level that we have never suspected. It can become a spiritual path that can lead us out of our mental division.

In a time of appearances, pretence and political spin, nothing can make us more real, grounded and balanced than taking a good look at *the other side* of what we consume and of who we think we are—and a nose-full of what is so well beyond our artificial self-images and public personae...

Anybody suffering from overweight, haemorrhoids, "terrible" smells, or disconnectedness from body or others, will take great benefit from such a journey of honest self-discovery and should never flush his pound of poo without knowing it first and saying hello...

Taking a dump should be a joy and is much improved by a good belly-laugh! In this spirit I would like to invite anybody who eats food onto a journey of self-knowledge that will reveal what goes on in the dark and that will inevitably lead to a true awareness of who we really are when the pants are down.

No disrespect towards any of the almost fictional characters in session is intended, even while clarity of expression must outweigh diplomatic correctness under such dire circumstances.

Without much doubt, dear reader, your head and your view of society and life will be severely challenged by reading this shit, and you may even feel sick or offended at some stage. Make the most of it! The truth will set you free, dramatically improve your health and evolve your consciousness...

Be ready—this is a book on real shit and on those realities, we never meant to face.

Chapter 1: Food and shit

Everything in the universe has two sides: Protons/electrons, up/down, inside/outside, male/female, yin/yang. Nothing can be understood without understanding the underlying duality of its oneness. Who would know what "left" means—if there is no "right?"

Shit and food are the two sides of the coin called "digestion!" Imagine a tube where we put a banana into one end and then it comes out the other end—changed! Transported from outside to inside and back to outside! We need to look at this entire process, not just at what we put in, if we are to understand the rules of the tube!

We have made food and dieting into a cult, where everybody knows exactly how many calories are in their burger. But our diets do not at all work—because we look only at the food-side of things, only at the in-put.

It does not matter so much how many nutrients we eat! What matters is how much of it we actually can make use of in the life-style we lead. This means that calorie-tables and general ideas on food are quite meaningless as they are unrelated to individual needs and personal temperament.

Whether strawberries for example are healthy or not depends on how well they are accepted by the individual mind/body and not at all on their analysis of nutrients.

Some people can eat cake as much as they want and stay skinny—and others gain weight by just thinking of cake! Calorie content does not come into it that much... All that matters is whether cake is an appropriate food for a specific person, under the circumstances!

The best way to find out which foods are suited and which are not is to examine what happens to those foods in the digestive tract! If they digest well, leaving no smells and no gas, forming a nice, light-brown, nearly floatable sausage—they are appropriate foods! If they come out as stinky green slime or hard, fast-sinking rocks and pebbles, they are the wrong food for that person, no matter what the general analysis of that food may proclaim.

Food alone however does not predict the quality of the shit it becomes. Shit is determined by food as well as by character, emotional states and the resulting digestive ability!

If you're nervous, or fearful, your peristaltic movements increase and you may get the runs... and if you hold onto your old convictions, you tend to constipate...

This being so observable, one wonders why it is not general knowledge and why doctors and scientists continue to exclude mind and emotion as the main factors as to what befalls the body...

Apart from the general taboo over all things anal, the reason for most of our problems with food is that eating has become the main pillar of consumerism, which underneath all else, emphasizes what we "take" over what we "give!"

Eating is the main manifestation of "taking" or "receiving" of energy from the outside and as such symbolizes the essence of what it is to be a consumer...

Eating and "evacuating" are on the physical level of reality what "receiving" and "giving" are on the mental and spiritual level! More than mere symbol, eating is the most fundamental form of receiving/taking from the outside there is, beside inhaling, drinking and tantric sex.

All of us love eating, receiving, taking, "having" sex and "having" a drink. What we, who are programmed to consume, don't like near as much is "giving" in all of its forms!

We don't like "letting go" near as much as we like controlling! We don't like "giving" sex as much as "having" it and we don't enjoy watering our plants quite as much as we enjoy having a drink for ourselves...

We don't like shitting near as much, as we do like eating...

Let's face it—as consumers we are basically selective and selfish people, who give only as much as absolutely necessary, and hope to receive it all!

Some may insanely think that we "deserve to have it all," but do we ever glimpse the "other side" of our title, the fact that somehow, sometime, we will have to give it all back in order to just survive?

Do we realize, when shopping for all those things we desire, that eventually they end up in landfills, as unmanageable mountains of rubbish, as chemical concentrations in our drinking water? No, we do not! We see only the new thing in the shop and the getting and having of it! Not the giving back of it! This is one main division created by consumerism and utterly unrecognized by its apostles. And this division affects not only our assimilation of food, but our entire view of the world!

Just as elemental as eating, breathing follows the same pattern—It may be easy to inhale, but exhaling, giving up the air and the "inside" to the "outside"—that has become very difficult for many! The medical labelling of this condition as "asthma," which is one of the most progressive diseases of our time and culture, does little to help us see the underlying cause. The disease is never examined in the context of how asthmatics feel and think and shit differently from others...

The inability to let go of air is psychologically very closely related to the inability to let go of shit, which is why asthmatics often also are constipated!

In matters of sexual and social exchange it is easy to see how a preference for "receiving" on all channels must forestall any true devotion or real love, which sufficiently explains our high divorce-rates and sexual deficiencies today.

But what truly takes the cake is when we finally look in the mirror! Our body-size leaves us flabbergasted, alienated and divorced from who we thought we were, and it overwhelms all other self-perception! Do we need plastic surgery? What else is there?

Well, there is the truth...

The fact to face is that our wonderful democratic societies have produced a culture of obese and selfish slobs, who take all they can for themselves, and who eat to fill up a growing emotional void—with physical food!

It is this deep affection with "taking" which now becomes our biggest downfall...we have taken so much—we can barely move! We have quite forgotten how and why to eat...!

When we want sex with a person, we ask them out to dinner! When we celebrate, we feast! When we're sad and alone, we eat for entertainment! Eating is *it*!

Now we gradually realize that on some level we have to start living with the consequences of this imbalance.

All extreme yin after a while becomes yang—and vice versa...

Eating has, with the growth of the fast "food" industry on one hand, and the beauty-industry on the other, become a guilty, sinful and shameful thing, at least subliminally. This does not stop us from eating ever more, but it stops us from enjoying food guilt free, happily, gratefully, and without greed! And those feelings are necessary to enjoy unproblematic exchange of energy!

If you are not grateful for your food, you will not digest it so well. If you feel guilty when eating, you will not allow the nutrients to nourish you well, your liver will suffer and excrete less potent digestive juices, your stomach-ph will not be quite so adaptable, nor will the gut-walls assimilate nutrients very efficiently. This is how emotions and thoughts constantly change and determine all bio-chemical processes in our bodies.

We now need to ask—Is there a cure to obesity, that does not only count calories but actually addresses the underlying, more fundamental issues?

Nature's own cure to eating is shitting! The cure to abnormal eating is to vomit or to face the shit such eating produces, and to smell it!

Our shit tells us more about a food than any dietary advice! Doctors are quite aware of the value of stool-analysis, and will agree that it gives the best clues for a personalized diet and can even indicate non-digestive illnesses. They know that "stool" should have a homogenous texture and a light-brown colour, no blood in it and no white colour. They prefer it without a heinous stench while they analyse its exact properties...

Stench itself is never tested or appreciated... But at home, where we may have no lab, we still have a nose and soon learn to tell which foods our bodies accept easily and which they digest poorly!

If left to rot, sugar becomes sour, so if our shit smells sour we need to avoid the undigested sugars, for now.

Rotting fat becomes rancid, so rancid smelling shit indicates undigested fats. An analysis from the doctor's lab will probably show a lipase-deficiency. He recommends taking the digestive enzyme and to quit eating the fat.

Rotting protein smells foul, like rotten eggs—so foul smell tells us we don't digest our protein well. To stop eating protein or to take papaya is of course not a cure, only symptom management. The cure is in understanding what "protein" represents on the mental and emotional plane, in itself and relative to the patient, and to learn to accept that which is being ignored or resisted or replaced.

While fat nourishes the emotional body, and carbohydrates mostly the mental body, proteins look after the physical body structure or your active, material self. This allows us to relate digestive deficiencies to the way we think, feel and act.

We can recognize by the size, colour, texture, shape, weight and smell of our shit which foods are appropriate for us and what personality type we are—If only we are willing to look at this *other side* of food and at the opposite of what we prefer to see!

Our life-lessons strongly manifest in what we make of our food, and the act of facing our shit can actually bring about a grounded inner path that leads to health, harmony and true self-knowledge.

It is all about seeing both sides of the coin!

To know what is right—makes you self-righteous.

But to know left *and* right—gives you orientation!

If you know your food in isolation from how it is digested, you may be able to cook, —but you know nothing of what that food means to your body.

If you know your food *and* your shit—you can see the harmony between the outside world and who you are inside! You then see actions in the light of consequences...

You are making first connections...

Chapter 2: The Fat-man

He made it in there, just before you turned up, your own need ballooning with anticipation in your lower self.

The locks turn and says "occupied" in red. You get ready to camp, a man without business or a loose woman to any walker-by with a business...

Inside the toilet-box a wild rumbling starts, like of a caged animal trying frantically to escape its confines! The box shakes, its walls trying to stay together, but moaning with the effort. The seat goes down hard, followed by a heavy weight squashing it to squeaks—and a long-suffering sigh after that.

You wait and listen to the proceedings. Nothing happens, except a comfort-shifting of heavy body and little moans of near-readiness. No newspaper, that's good!

Then, when you start speculating on having missed a quiet, delicately mastered slide, an almighty splosh!—and two nearly as weighty after-sploshes end all your doubts and idle speculations!

Unbelievably, another aftershock thunders down the porcelain, followed by a sigh of final comfort.

You may feel a little constipated yourself at this stage or even envious, but you have to respect those forces of nature on display.

You hear toilet paper being torn out and plenty of shifting of weight and then the aroma gets to you, from under the door, and above, the sides, telling you all about what the man has eaten the previous day, what he mal-digested, what kind of life-style he leads...

There is a strongly under-oxygenated odour, as from an animal that has never been allowed outside. You remember a similar smell from the zoo, of freedom lost...

There is a note of rancidity in this waft, which explains the amount of toilet-paper needed to prevent fatty smears left behind...

You know from the sound alone, that none of those heavy sausages exceed twenty cm, in which case they'd just slide, not fall. This means the texture isn't so good. A big eater with good digestion can produce very long sausages that can curl several times to fill up half the bowl! No, here we have sausages that sink and smear, dropping like bombs without the slightest attempt at staying afloat. An eater of much fatty food, this man does not move much or breathe properly. He is a fat-man, spending his life sitting, his sex-life at the dinner-table, and his money on poor quality food.

If you have a little instinct left intact from the old days, the smell brings you even deeper visions:

There is a lack of originality, of freedom! Not a freethinker, definitely...the man takes it as it is given to him. He uncritically takes any food on offer, whether it is real food or crap in wrap...

He actually takes and accepts all his societal concepts as well, and all of the beliefs of his culture, and he thinks he is nothing but the body!

His philosophy of materialism came to him without further reflection, like all other postulates he receives from the outside world. His father's son...

The fat-man does not give of his true inner self, does not share his doubts and real feelings. He prefers to talk about your feelings, not his! The outside and the physical are too dominant to allow a personal perspective...

He is the perfect citizen, manifesting faithfully all those beliefs his society puts to him. He is not responsible for his own world view! He is as obedient as parents and school taught him to be and he doesn't burn many calories over questioning the comfortable.

However, all things eventually move towards their opposite! The man who conforms so completely to society is getting pushed to its fringe, since to be or not to be "fat" has become a hallmark of success or failure, and a huge factor in the forming of self-image...

To be or not to be fat has become the new existential question in the western world, and many hate fat people because they so remind them of their own impending future.

Not wanting to share their predicament, they blame fat people for having no discipline and for eating all day.

There is however a collective psychological reason for obesity that goes much deeper than eating too much, and this reason goes a long way to explain why no diet works and why fat people find it so difficult to lose any weight despite debilitating fasts and chemical warfare!

This reason is nearly as impossible to discover while living in a consumer society as it is for fish to discover water—and has therefore never been considered.

The true reason for our obesity epidemic is our collective and absolute belief in "growth"- in maximised material growth of business and economy!

There is in itself nothing wrong with a philosophy of "growth" or with the physical perspective. Nature herself teaches us of constant growth. Things either grow or die.

But have we really grown things like the gardener is growing healthy food? Observant of the cycles of nature? And—have we ever happily given back to the Earth??

And have we grown our inner selves as well, like the good gardener, realizing how our very essence wants to grow, grow up to be something, along with the things we grow outside ourselves?

No, we haven't!

We only evolve matter, not humanity! "Our" progress is a progress of matter only! Technology is purely material, external and unconcerned with the workings of mind or soul.

And we don't grow at natural rates either—we grow as fast as we possibly can, in all the superficial areas of life, wherever we actually can do so...

Instead of respecting the natural growth rates, like of forests, we grow at the expense of those forests. We take far too much fish from the oceans, giving nothing back and we destroy hundreds of life-forms by growing into their habitats. We have not been the gardener, but a parasite in our collectively shared habitat!

We have taken far too much and given nothing back! Are we not greedy and selfish buggers whose main faith is in the continuation of such uncontrolled growth during our own lifetime?

The reason for this blindness and its existence-threatening consequences is that we never looked at 'the other side' of this growth, which is—destruction and death!

The forest does not only constantly grow, but it also constantly dies! All the growing trees rot back into the soil. There is death everywhere!

In society and in the body the same universal laws apply as in the forest: more growth—more death and destruction...

But while growth is intended and embraced, destruction is ignored or not even recognized! Destruction as in the eradication of forests, waterways, landscapes, air, drinking water, the running out of resources on which our excessive growth is based...and of course—cancer!

We think we can just choose the nice part of the duality growth/destruction and get away with it! Restrict the destruction part to third world countries and to other species...

This is possibly the gravest error of our time!

Our religious faith in material growth (without death...) naturally also affects our bodies, our material selves!

Body simply follows mind. You believe in growth—and your body will obey!

Mind (genes, previous life) creates body in the first place and continues to shape the body in its image. Fearful, aggressive or selfless incarnations (foetuses) develop fearful, aggressive or selfless head-shapes, as phrenology clearly shows. The soul, via the genes, decides what pigmentation your irises will have, and also your blood and your DNA are a direct manifestation of who you are as a non-physical being.

Hormones are just another word for "feelings," not anything else. If you get over your anger (adrenaline) by understanding, your adrenaline levels will immediately drop...

And if you avoid all thought of death and destruction, your body will grow disproportionately, as it is not balanced by a sufficient "astral" restraint!

We refuse to accept responsibility for what "happens" to us and we do not want to see how we make ourselves ill, how we get our head-aches, have accidents, ruin our lungs, how we attain genetic deficiencies...we see all that as an arbitrary fate or blame it on our genes...

By labelling our growing mental disorders, from anorexia to PMS or allergy as diseases—we are no longer personally responsible! The doctors are! The "disease" is!

To suggest that fat people are the result of their own creation, not that of calories, is in our day highly "politically incorrect," but therefore that much more necessary to state.

Instead of staying hypnotized by the counting of calories and by Jenny Craig's lost stomachs, we must simply take responsibility and remember that we are inner beings and not purely physical or statistical machines...

What happens when we, not just individually but collectively, believe in maximal growth and at the same time see ourselves mostly as "the body"??

Aiming collectively at eight per cent growth per year, and wanting to *expand* as soon as possible—this thinking and such a belief will inevitably make our bodies grow! Especially when our business finds it too hard to achieve!

What we also overlook is how we as individuals are affected by this attitude of unchecked and maximised growth...

Does this growth include growth in consciousness? Growth in ethical awareness? Growth in ability for peace? Growth in our humanity? Does it?

Have we grown as human beings as we have grown our businesses? Isn't it rather that we have developed only the outside, our comfort, our bank account, our wardrobe...?

Our total belief in growth is not only cultural, but manifests as a determination to expand our own culture beyond all bounds, at the expense of other cultures! We are the global fat-man, who grows his own culture like a cancer into the tissue of the global fabric of all other human cultures, believing it more important than all else...Such beliefs always affect the body, using its metaphorically precise language of change...

As individuals, we have defined growth as material, external and physical, just as we have as a society! Such growth can only be of the body, by definition.

Our bodies grow in obedience to our cultural beliefs in maximized growth!

This is why people in countries like New Zealand, the US, England or Germany gain weight no matter what diet they follow or how much they plan to eat!

And because they do not want to be "losers," they find it nearly impossible to lose that extra weight later...

If we diet, forcing down our calorie intake, we will not lose any weight long-term! Fasting makes our digestion far more efficient, and eventually we will need much less food to maintain the same weight!

Our metabolism adjusts to fasting and when our fast is over, we regain our previous weight within days. Everybody with dieting experience knows that. It has recently been proven that some people can gain weight by even thinking of food...so no—calorie-intake does not deserve our exclusive attention! That approach can never work! We need to correct our minds, not just the body!

We need to remember that our mind regulates physical processes!

Without adjusting and learning the real lesson, without letting go of our religion of maximal growth, we will get fatter and bigger, until our bodies far outweigh sanity and spirit.

Our collective "body," the economy, needs exactly the same fix, and giving a trillion dollars to help the finance companies does not address the real problems, which are—greed, division and the avoidance of our true inner selves for maximized profit and the fantasy of unlimited growth!

Our faith in uncontrolled physical growth is killing us individually and culturally, unless we start facing our shit and the 'death' that comes with growth!

A beginning in dealing with that would be to stop feeding our children yesterday's crap, to stop measuring only their bodily growth, and to cease encouraging them to want ever more things, toys, clothes and food...

We need to remind ourselves that life is not a race for more material, and that our children need to be nurtured emotionally and spiritually, not just shown the way to the fridge and to material success...

The fat-man needs to re-define "growth" as personal, not physical! He needs to recover his freedom and get out of the cage! Out of the box he is in! The walls of his box consist of his full obedience to collective and cultural norms he never questions...

To free himself from this globalized new religion of *maximum material growth* and its psycho-physiological effects, he has to want that freedom and bear its solitude.

The meditations fly away with the opening of a window...

Smells and intuitions dissipate and diminish...

You just hope the guy comes out of the box, but are less than certain you want to be going next into that same box.

Twenty litres of water flushing the deposited grenades down the gurgler...

The toilet door rumbling to life, he says "vacant" and out comes the fat-man—a twelve to thirteen-year-old boy, moving along with his heavy body, back to the life he is leading, glad of the temporary emptiness, but hungry already, for he cannot guess what...

Chapter 3: The anorexic girl

Her sittings take as long as the fat-man's. She tries to give the little she has taken, but it is hard to give what she hasn't really got. A bit like the exhalation of an asthmatic, who has never taken a proper breath or a catholic priest talking of sex.

The pebbles she often produces suggest she is holding on to something, an idea of control, of being still in charge. The doctor will tell her that hard "stool" comes from too little fluid and from a loss of peristaltic movement caused by insufficient practise and this is quite so. The slime that often comes with the pebbles is produced by the body to facilitate "evacuation." But it also betrays a deep division...

Instead of shitting homogenously textured sausages, there is a conflict between two opposites that she can't reconcile. She dangles between these opposites and can't find her own integrating way, can't escape the conflict of either/or!

She struggles so hard that blood is regularly in her defecations, showing the depth of her hurt, her self-inflicted pain and misdirected anger.

She feels very alone, but she is not—anorexia is a cultural epidemic much like obesity and progressively eats its way mostly through the female half of the population in consumer countries.

Anorexics quite often also have asthma and haemorrhoids, finding the letting go of breath as hard as are their pellets. But what is it that the anorexic girl cannot accept and assimilate and simply will not surrender? Are her mental difficulties an arbitrary "fate," or specific to the errors she commits? What has anorexia to do with a cultural psyche that produces it so excessively?

No doctor is treating anorexia as a cultural mental illness, which would be the only way to address the problem systematically and to find permanent cure! Doctor just tells her to eat more, making her instantly sick and uninterested in doctors...

She withdraws from useless "help," which includes her parents...

What help is there for her that would get to the root of this mental disorder?

The anorexic girl sees what the fat-man cannot see where our cultural religion of "growth" is concerned! She is disgusted by it—by how people eat, by what they eat, by their fatness and by her being a part of this same culture!

She rebels against what actually requires a rebellion!

The problem for her is that she is not strong enough within herself to be a rebel or to stand alone against society (parents!). She is young, of a child-like immaturity, and her self-esteem does not allow her to take a psychological position of "I'm okay, you're not okay." Who then does she rebel against, if rebel she must?

Against herself of course, who else? What else could she successfully control?

She hates herself for ever participating in the gluttony and boundless excesses of her "eat-all-you can" culture, so she says no—in a shy and misguided way...

There is however one thing she absolutely shares with the fat-man—a belief in the physical, in the body and in body-image!!

More even than the fat-man, she sees herself exclusively as "the body," and subscribes to all those Barbie-doll images and fashion demands and to knowing herself through the mirror and through other people's perception—even if she calls herself "spiritual."

When a "normal" person looks into the mirror, they see much the same as what others would also see—the body as it is. But if you relate only to body-image, denying or overlooking all other parts of self, those suppressed parts do not just evaporate, but find their way into that mirror, mixing with the perception of body! For this reason, the anorexic sees in the mirror not only the body, but also that hidden personality, which is a "fat" participant in a culture that she cannot truly distance herself from, and that still influences how she sees herself.

She sees herself as fat because she sees her cultural mind in the mirror, not just her body!

Her inner person is "fat," as it is still aligned with her culture, her parents, the streets full of fast-food outlets, and she perceives this inner person as physical, since that is at the bottom of her shared materialistic world-view, and all she can see.

If you believe in the primacy of body, but not in growth—the body will have to diminish.

The anorexic girl is hypnotised by the physical aspect of reality and conducts her rebellion on a purely physical plane. Part of this is her subscription to drugs which put all emotions down to a physical/chemical cause that need not be owned.

Anorexic girls do not make good business women, nor do their bank accounts tend to grow, which they put down to being soulful or "spiritual." They detest growth in all its forms, like profit-thinking or expansion of business, or moving into a bigger house—not to mention pregnancy!

Their perception deteriorates towards seeing nothing but the body, which leads them to reject all else about who they really are. If you always see the physical, how could you still perceive and respect things emotional or personal? These parts of self then cease to be relevant...

Anorexics are often quite intelligent (capable of consistent thought), but exhibit a huge gulf between theory and action. This leads to guilt...

The anorexic is much more difficult to cure than the fat-man, since her non-intellectual self is so hard to approach and because of her basic insincerity.

Worse still is the situation for the bulimic girl, who does not even mean a real *no* towards what she finds "disgusting." Instead, the bulimic fully participates in orgies of feeding and consuming, only to feel massively guilty and disgusted with herself immediately afterwards.

Not having the strength of character to say no and walk her own path, the bulimic girl hypocritically says *no* only when she is not challenged to act upon it, when it is all theory—like right after a feeding bout! Her *no* lasts only a short time, she never means it for long or for real.

She cannot really let go of her consumer-self, only of the food she has eaten—a classical transference.

Her rejection of food and self becomes paramount, obsessive (only option seen), secretive (does not want this confronted) and guilty.

Vomiting her food back onto the table could be a positive step to take from a shamanic point of view—since it invites the family to deal together with their skinny girl with what exactly is on the table, to confront the exact face of the daughter's disgust—the sour, spoilt love smell of it! Accept this *Gestalt* and there is no further need for secrecy...

But she throws up secretly, privately, no longer a part of her family. Her rebellion can and must not be manifest, not expressed against her loving parents, who to teenagers sometimes still represent society or *the world*.

The more suppressed this inner rejection is, the more secret it becomes, and self-esteem goes to hell.

Bulimics are not often capable of being consistent or trustworthy, nor do they trust themselves as far as they can throw up. Alternating between feeding and vomiting, between theory and opposite action, between being a mindless consumer and experiencing the disgust of it—there is no possible ground for self-acceptance!

The world is a battle-ground, and the girl a helpless victim of a disease! She cannot happily participate in the *world*, nor can she live without it.

Her thoughts are generally about the physical body, but she is extremely head-centred and mostly un-physical.

In a hunter/gatherer society she could not survive except by leaning on her community. Her lack of responsibility would be addressed as such, instead of as a new "disease." She would face a work-load she can only survive by eating correctly...

But natural societies do not produce anorexics in the first place, nor did anorexia exist at all a few hundred years ago.

It is very difficult to "help" a bulimic, as they won't take responsibility for self and will require a maturing and strengthening of character that school and parents have not managed to bring about. They need self-responsible action!

Talking gets us nowhere with the bulimic. She will agree with all you put to her, without making it her own. She just ignores it. Her secrecy makes her very dishonest. Medicine is of little help here. She needs character-building in a practical, non-mental, physical environment, where she cannot get away with lies, theories and escapes!

She needs to see growth where she can appreciate it, as in a forest, and she needs to discover her real self in a mirror-less, un-cluttered and real world, where her body is not something to look at or to judge, but where she works hard for a living and feels the self-respect that goes with physical activity!

Inside a western consumer world, the bulimic will almost never be cured. Her "stool" symbolizes the duality, the split in her reality. There is no integration between hard pebbles and watery slime, only this and that, no integrated sausage, no conclusions.

Eat—fast. Eat—vomit. Participate—reject... There is never any congruence between how she feels and how she acts, only a heated alternation between opposites, which makes her deeply unhappy and is very detrimental to her self-respect.

To heal the bulimic girl, she needs to come out of her head first, which is an alien concept to medical science. She needs to learn several things from nature:

That eating and growing can be good acceptable things.

That she is not just the body.

That she is not an outcast, not "wrong" or "bad" for not accepting part of her culture, like eating bad food for fun or from boredom.

She needs to take responsibility for herself, her own world view and act accordingly in a self-reliant environment.

Crossing Canada with a hunting bow would do it, or sailing a boat single-handedly for a month...

People who have learned to respect food, from having known real hunger (as in not getting food when you really want it...), never over-eat or throw up perfectly good food!

We are looking at a cultural disease, a mental disorder, stemming from our alienation from a balanced, natural life—but individually it always remains a choice!

Even for the ordinary or slight anorexic a true cure must consist in facing and clearing the underlying errors, in maturing of character and in being self-responsible, particularly for eating and speaking only what is needed, appreciated, and easily respected!

To meditate on her shit in the literal sense is for the heady anorexic a highly effective technique to discover that which has been ignored and left to a subliminal level! To look at her shit, and smell it too, she needs to overcome tremendous emotional resistance, but if she can do it, an awareness beyond thinking seeps into her mind which grounds her immediately and can lead to insight and a true rehabilitation of her person.

Looking at shit brings her out of the head, and smelling it without disgusted withdrawal even more so, shifting awareness away from the superficial and visual, towards accurate grounded and honest perception.

To be aware of her shit is of course a great therapy against secrecy and avoidance too!

When she vomits, she should meditate on *what was once part of her*, before cleaning it off the table! People don't do that for very long...

Becoming more aware of her emotional and mental self and fostering an attitude of growth in those areas, must go hand in hand with a reduction in visual body perception!

Secrecy can only be addressed by cultivating honesty and openness, just as self-responsibility is encouraged by respect and self-respect.

Anorexia goes with a life- and spirit-threatening world-view, more akin to suicide than to a disease, and needs to be understood as a possible and likely response to our collectively held attitudes of eating all we can. Where obese people conform to their programming to grow, the anorexic secretly defies this program and can't lose enough flesh to sufficiently express their contempt for it!

The fat-man and the anorexic girl are the Janus-faces of a greed-based consumer-psyche, where one obediently says *yes* and grows, and the other says a weak and powerless *no*, and shrinks. Both are equally brainwashed by materialist world-views into making their body-sizes the main or exclusive stage for their psychological conflicts.

If you are anorexic—you're controlling the wrong thing!

Leave your body uncensored and un-pierced and chemically unaltered! Why punish or reduce your body, when it could be your temple of joy? Do consistent, hard physical work and eat what you feel you need!

Get out of your head, live in the country and go for long walks in the forest!

Keep fast and slower-growing house-plants, if you need to be indoors. They grow on you, so be responsible for their well-being and grow along-side them!

Discover your body's ability to give you sexual pleasure, not just to others, and never feel guilty afterwards...

Respect your body, respect food—and you may learn to respect even yourself!

Then you can start to discover who you are where you are not the body.

Chapter 4: "I love my meat"

The fat lady in the cubicle next to mine has finally settled.

Her powerful chemical perfume hasn't!

It hit me hard when first she entered, but now it is overwhelming...

Her bulk must be muting the sounds of production or else she tries very hard to suppress her moans and efforts. Anyhow—here comes the slosh of a good pound slapping solidly against the porcelain, and another for good measure. Not bad.

Then it happens. A sharp, foul stench creeps through the chemical curtain, overpowering even the cheap sweet perfume, and crawls inexorably down my throat, like a soup of rotten eggs, to stifle my breath and ending my desire to be here now...

What we are facing here, is a person who eats a lot of protein, but does not use it up by working her muscles, excreting the undigested protein. Could be a dieter, drinking protein shakes and skipping the gym, but the slap of her pound of poop was a little too solid for that.

No, here is a woman who "loves her meat," eating hamburgers for breakfast, sausages for lunch and steak for dinner. But she doesn't like to move...

She is a city-girl at home or with a cosy desk-job, never does any physical work (except now...).

She considers sport to be dangerous and verbalizes aggression as sarcasm.

You can smell all that quite easily. It is the same difference in smell you will find between a wild animal and a caged one fed on power-food; full of stagnant, suppressed energy, toxic, foul and devoid of the freshness of life.

This smell of foul rot is a consequence of eating more meat than is used up by the muscles and as such a message to correct protein intake or increase physical activity.

This message is however not received! It is hidden under a sweetish perfume, designed to mask the deeper truth and to avoid the necessity to make corrections.

Everything about this lady is camouflage: she politely cloaks her aggressions, hides her weaknesses in full sight, and even the sounds trying to escape during her business in the 'bathroom' are censored. She does not like you watching her eat all those burgers, nor does she like you to look at or talk about her body. She will get surprisingly aggressive if you probe into any of the many things she avoids thinking about. But when in control, she puts on a sweet fragrance, a sweet personality and feeds other people roasts and pastries.

Her tendency to suppress aggression can bring her stomach ulcers and late divorces.

The perpetual semi-digested protein in her gut can lead to severe imbalances in the type of bacteria inhabiting the bowels and consequently to bowel disease.

For this personality, eating meat is not a good idea, unless she does the hunting and skinning, the butchering and preparing of the meat also.

There is nothing wrong, in principle, about eating meat, but meat-eating is connected to a hunter's life-style, or a body-builder's or a carpenter's! If we eat meat like a labourer while sitting in an office or at home, watching TV—then meat becomes toxic.

After a while, those enzymes necessary to digest meat degenerate and we now digest incompletely. Our shit starts to stink.

Many new-age philosophers equate meat-eating with low consciousness or with ignorant aggression, thinking it unhealthy and un-spiritual! The gurus in India all seem to agree on that as well. Without a doubt, they are quite correct as far as they themselves are concerned. Philosophers and gurus don't hunt or butcher animals or build houses and bodies! If you sit in meditation much of the time, in a hot country, or stroll along the beach in contemplation of the divine—meat does not suit you! It would be toxic to such a person, especially in tropical heat!

But is meat as such "bad" for your health?

There can never be a yes or no answer to such a question. It is all relative to who you are and to what meat it is and what you are eating it for.

In a culture where chickens and pigs are raised in economically tight cages, and under very cruel and brutal conditions suffer intolerable lives—certainly such a meat is not fit to eat.

Where cows are injected and fed antibiotics and chemicals supposed to replace our nutrient-deficient soils—such a meat is not fit to eat!

And since we reject all the thousands of other meats that are not as yet polluted and genetically engineered, we can quite rightfully say that all meat available from the butcher is "bad" for you.

The health statistics bear that out, too, and doctor will often advise against eating meat.

The truth about meat is however far removed from what doctors discuss and from what people believe.

The first problem is that we are missing the right questions! Whether meat is "bad" for you is a question in need of some clarification, before it can be answered intelligibly.

Meat is definitely "bad" for you if it is polluted in industrial food production! So avoid beef, pork and chickens together with all cultural programming that limits what we recognize as edible meat to a handful of domestically abused animals!

Go travel to Thailand and try the many crisp insects you find at the Chiang Mai and other markets!

Snack away on grasshoppers, crickets and fried beetles to enjoy some really high-quality meat without sprays, anti-life pills or growth hormones!

Try the frogs in Bali or their smoked ducks...

The deepest understanding about meat can clearly be found in the Philippines: "We eat all animals and all parts of every animal," Oscar told me when preparing to quick-roast a cow-hide he had marinated in local spices and boiled for three days, then cut into strips. It popped up like crackling crossed with popcorn and tasted like no meat I'd ever tried. Fantastic!

We ate dogs (never our family dog, no Filipino does that!) in vinegar, bay and juniper, and plenty of iguanas, bats, anything alive and around. The chickens, pigs and dogs were free, happy and in a natural, coconut-eating environment...

Enjoying good wild meats in great variety is absolutely not unhealthy!

And as all Native American hunters stand to witness—eating meat goes perfectly well with a highly evolved spirituality! Just don't kill what you don't eat and don't eat what you never killed...

It is unhealthy to eat only the meat of three or four animals, yes, just as it is unhealthy to eat only three or four vegetables. If we only ever ate wheat, potatoes and tomatoes, we would soon mal-digest corn, millet, carrots and all else. We would suffer mineral imbalances and deficiencies and get ill.

As it is important to give the body a great variety of fruit, vegetables and grains, it is just as important to give it a large selection of meat animals.

The most important point to make about the quality of meat however is that we always eat the same type of meat—muscle flesh! We usually eat one specific body-part of an animal all the time! When we eat steak, we always eat just the muscle of the back of a cow! No predator does that! Not one. They all eat the "steaks" last!

It is just like living on wheat after throwing all the good parts, germ and bran, away. Oh yeah, we do that too, don't we?

Interesting is that nutritionists and even holistic food experts are so informed as far as plants and grains go, but collectively ignore to apply the same holistic insights to meat...

Eating only the back-muscle of cows is the biggest deviance from natural behaviour we exhibit around eating meat!

It is natural (ask any dog), to eat the inner organs first, starting with the liver!

It is natural to any predator to eat the brain, break the bones for the delicious marrow and chew the bones themselves for bits of cartilage.

What makes us think we can so dramatically deviate from these predator ways? That we are not really a predator? Think again! Evolution thinks in millions of years...

Just as we get sick from eating white bread and pasta instead of whole grain, we also get sick from eating only muscle and no liver, no lungs, no kidneys, no hearts, no marrow!

Only the effects are much worse, as they remain unseen by scientists looking through their cultural lenses...

We are what we eat, in a way. Eating muscle, we eat effort, struggle, conscious work, aggression, movement, fear, escape, tension, quick growth. Muscles can grow very large compared to other body-parts and this hormone-driven growth is what we eat—all the time. We think our rat-race towards "success" requires beef for fuel, but such causalities usually work in reverse as well—eating muscle causes us to compete and to fight, to run from feelings of fear and to generally tense up.

As usual, the fault lies with our own ignorance, caused by division, not in the thing we point at as the scapegoat. If you eat all parts of many types of animal, respecting those animals and their life-styles, then eating meat is just wonderful and brings no problems to a working body or spirit!

After clarifying what we mean by "meat," we now need to figure out who *we* are.

If you are a person tending to obesity, red face and neck, or exuding "foul" smells, then meat is not a good food for your personal needs!

If you're highly strung, aggressive, restless, domineering, then meat is not good. For you!

But if you're the skinny, pale vegetarian type, the thinker without much strength, or if you need to do heavy physical work—meat is not only good and necessary, but the best medicine nature is offering...You always get strong doses of iron from red meat, which represents strength!

To know what is good for you personally, you need to consciously look at your shit!

How do shape and colour and weight change when you eat meat and when you don't? What is the smell like?

Do what your poo tells you to do...be responsive.

Use your instincts and your own common sense, not what you've read!

Don't eat that pork from the super-market, because an unhappy pig that can't ever move around, nor see a blade of grass in its life, although injected against all the consequences of cruelty and disease, will make you share all those horrible emotions! They secrete hormonally into the flesh and the blood, just before you eat it! If you are at all "what you eat," then you'll be an utterly depressed person, without any joy of life...Quite appropriate really, that we should become like our victims...All victimization is self-victimization.

To choose that kind of meat is to lack all self-responsibility or awareness! It is insane and revolting. And the way we smell announces this to all creatures we meet.

But a fresh deer-liver, roasted on a stick, with onions...that is a health-food!

Nutritional value has very little to do with calories and chemical analysis. Nutritional value is in the life force! A happy, wild pig, shot to be eaten, may have the same calories, fat content and protein content as the deeply depressed one in the cage, but what do you think matters more here??

Look at what matters! Compare battery-eggs with happy farm-eggs and see what matters, beyond all the "scientific" eye-wash about calories and nutrients...

It is never about whether to eat or not to eat meat, eggs, milk or whatever, but about being able to discriminate between a clean, good food and—bad shit!

Here is where I join the fat lady's song— "I love my meat!" Thanks to my parents, who were foresters and hunters, raising me exclusively on meats from wild animals and home-grown foods, I grew up more like a jungle boy than like the average Bavarian youth ...

The meats I still love most are—sour deer liver, sour deer lungs (with Speckknödel), roast mallard duck, quail, pigeon, pheasant, pigeon stomach soup, quick-fried liver of fallow deer, stag testicles, raw deer tartar, tripe and onions, marinated and boiled deer tongues....

Today, I really love pork from those coconut-fed black pigs, tied to a coconut-tree on a long rope, and sweet/sour possum and... Anyway, you get the point what I mean by holistic meat-eating!

You see, "holistic" means wholesome in all areas, not just a few selected ones... ...and to never smell like eaters of supermarket flesh do, except a little after the raw tartar...as any dog would, unless he runs all day.

No, gurus be dammed! Enjoy your meat and forget about giving it up for any conceptual health- or "spiritual" reasons whatsoever! Meat is good. If you can get good meat that is!

And what about the act of the killing we call for when ordering meat? Is there "bad karma" in that? This is where Geronimo, the Apache, laughs out loud, knowing that killing is necessary, natural and good, if done in a grateful, graceful, and conscious way, for food!

Pale vegetarians are definitely not more spiritual than were the Apache or Sioux or Comanche! May the Great Spirit save us from such vain illusion!

I once listened to a somewhat "advanced" "Hare Krishna," who suggested that cows are sacred and must therefore not be killed and that the taking of any life is bad karma. So, he said, meat is bad...

He also said, after asserting that life is eternal, that the body is nothing but a shell...

I chose to challenge this and suggested that *all* animals are sacred, not just the cow (watch the division!). I offered that "killing" was according to him a mere "shedding of the shell" before the next incarnation, and no harm done to the cow's eternal wanderings...

And I asked him why he thinks lettuce plants a non-life, the eating of which does not kill...Has a carrot less life than a snail? Watch this arbitrary division I said, and the contradictions...

The good man had no coherent words after that. Maybe he realized that such mental concepts have very little to do with true awareness...

Hunters know more about meat and life than thinkers and vegetarians. They have the right grateful attitude and know what good meat is. The scientists and their followers don't.

The lady in her cubicle next to mine does not choose good meat; that is a fact!

And she eats a lot more than can be her fair share after a hunt...

She does not kill, but tears the flesh apart with her teeth like any predator.

She cannot digest all that meat very well, nor can the kidneys clean out those toxic hormones, the antibiotics, the growth hormones given with feed and the general unhappiness of a miserable life on death-row. So, her shit stinks like the murder she never herself committed. Underneath and in between her perfume, which announces secrecy and suppression, dwells toxic rot.

The more she keeps secretly hidden deep inside, the more it stinks when it comes out eventually. And the more she tries to cover it up with sweetness, the fouler the foulness becomes in contrast...

With hardly a sound apart from the flush, she is done and out of there, washing hands.

I can't see her, but I know she is applying lip-stick and more perfume, adjusting her robes and face to meet public expectation, then exits quickly, gently closing the door, forgetting to open the window. No Hindu that one...

Chapter 5: Love turned sour

I'm sitting on a white-man toilet on Malapascua Island, Philippines. I know the Manila-lady who has warmed up my seat. Restaurant owner; eating Filipino sweets all day, and sipping fruit-shakes...no family here, husband in Europe.

There's no window, all open to the breeze under the nipa-roof, and yet my liver cringes with the "odeur vinaigre" that lingers like an obsessive love...

I ponder how the sourness of her shit can so parallel the disappointed, drawn lines in her face and around her down-turned mouth... There is still some of that famous Filipino sweetness left, but most of it has seen too many pesos, too much city-life and too much agitation—and turned sour.

Love is sweet. And when the love is not there, we take to sweets to keep things sweet...

To this lady, love is *a good feeling* of sweet taste! That is of course not how life and love really are, but she does not know that, does not want to know that. She will keep things sweet to balance her disappointment and her sour face for as long as she can...

She eats sweets to maintain the *good feeling* under all circumstances. When she feels sad, when things go wrong, when she is lonely or simply bored—sugar will fix it...

Here is the basic problem: sugar does not fix these emotional needs, it just makes them invisible, persistent and thus addictive!

If she ate dried mangos, bananas and coconuts to sweeten her life up a little, she would not be in trouble. But Filipinos use really large amounts of white sugar (those who can afford it), which is one of the greatest killers of our "civilization..."

It is mostly a problem of cultural deterioration and of overnight changes in people's psyche.

I have lived in Asia and Polynesia for years and witnessed an inability in culturally destabilized people to cope with sugar and alcohol, which is fermented sugar, in all of these places.

The most terrible form of a disturbed replacement of *good feeling* with sugar is the diabetes epidemic that sweeps those native peoples as soon as they come into contact with sweet "civilization!"

In the mountain tribes, where roads, electricity and even the white man haven't yet arrived, there is no diabetes as far as I've seen.

There are no unloved or lonely people. Everybody is a member of a very large family and when he gets old he is respected, looked after and honoured as the venerable head of a large family. Nobody will put him into any retirement home.

Life is sweet, even if white people call that "poor," and there is never a lack of love or any inability to accept and assimilate being loved.

When the white man comes, big families start breaking up, kids go off to Manila, tourists and business people from the city come in and create new values in dollars.

Malapascua is such a place. Much of it is still quite untouched, but where the tourists lodge, the life-style of local people has completely changed.

Kids, who just recently were content to throw coins and drive bicycle-tyres with a stick, are now watching TV and American war- and crime-movies. They want a motor-bike and a mobile phone and they want to be "hot." So they're heating up, fuelled by highly sugared cokes and alcohol (poison to Filipinos...) and then revolt against their parents and against their ancient family values.

Family, forever the highest value to any Filipino, starts to crumble...

The embeddedness in family and love, that Filipinos and also Polynesians always had to rely on and that stabilizes their psychological well-being, is getting lost for many and often very suddenly.

It was very noticeable in Malapascua, where about every second middle-aged person I was introduced to, seemed to have diabetes.

So I went to the cemetery and found that fifty years ago, people normally died in their eighties. The freshest graves however mostly held locals who died in their fifties...

Talking to Filipinos with diabetes I found them still loved by their families, but they themselves could not assimilate that love as they used to. This is often alcohol-driven, where a decision for selfish pleasure is made against the wishes of family, or by touching the city-life in Manila, but most commonly by virtue of tourism.

In all cases, the loss of family, love and culture is being compensated for by eating white sugar and by drinking sugar in the shape of rum! Soon the growing inability to receive and handle love starts then to affect the function that connects back to the physical plane—the assimilation of sugary food...

Diabetes is one way for the body to express how cultural change can impact on sugar-digestion. The other, more common dysfunction is in simply not digesting sugars well, which leads to sour shit.

Where in diabetes the love is still received, but not assimilated and balanced, sour shit points to love turned sour and rejected, and also to love being replaced and as such not acceptable to the body.

A cultural dysfunction should of course be culturally addressed, not just individually.

It is much harder for a Filipino or Samoan to step outside their cultural reality than it is for a westerner, since it is family that ties them to their cultural beliefs so much more.

Christianity has shaped their beliefs and concepts of love with religious dogma that threatens hell, damnation and utter isolation from family and community, if not lived up to!

Modern Filipinos or Samoans who have worked in New Zealand, simply cannot live up to these values any more, after spending their money gambling, watching Hollywood movies and living in their own flat. They miss their families terribly and try to improve how they feel with alcohol and sugar, which they cannot handle, because that is not *it*. They see themselves as somewhat unloving for leaving their family and as selfish for living their new lives.

Naturally, they will then "love" their children by feeding them with sweets, much as we do in the West, when we have little time or real love to give...

With native peoples, a loss of family and love through cultural deterioration, in combination with the availability of sugar, definitely lies at the root of diabetes and mal-digestion of sugar.

The situation is not much different in the western world, where even our normal working day keeps us well away from our loved ones and from a consistent exchange of loving. When we then retire from work, our "loved ones" put us into retirement homes, cutting off all real love... Some people cannot handle that very well!

Our nuclear families keep us away from our extended family. Anybody who has lived in an extended tribal family knows how poor our nuclear families are in terms of security, old age isolation and how dependant the children are of their absentee fathers or stressed-out mothers and how removed from older people.

What children get instead of family love, like money, toys and sugar, cannot be perfectly digestible emotionally, because it is not the real thing!

If we feed them chocolate, cakes and lollypops to be "content" and "happy"—how can we possibly expect that to work? Their bodies then try to correct the error or make us aware of it. But we can't see that, since we don't expect the body to have any such wisdom.

Then their poo changes towards sour—and we still notice nothing...

Happiness and love simply cannot be bought in shops! This presents a certain difficulty for the consumer used to buying all he needs out there in some shop! Avoiding the real issue, the feeling of lost love and lacking safety, and to replace an emotional need by transferring it to the physical plane like in sugar or rum, is a falseness that will always manifest on the bodily or physical level as a falsification of the body's digestive response!

From a feeling of "missing love," the diabetic moves towards a growing inability to feel that any longer, which then inhibits the production of insulin.

Some people can accept this replacement for years and simply become bigger and fatter before they eventually develop diabetes, while others become sugar-intolerant early, get fluctuating blood-sugar levels, or just shit real sour.

Usually, people who gain weight, find their isolation from family and community increasing dramatically! This loss of accepting love often tips them into diabetes!

That happens when they subconsciously recognize that sugar is not helping the real need and yet keep eating it because it is all the love they can get...

The body however never tolerates being cheated for long. You cannot hide truth from your body!

When sugar is found out to be something other than love, the body starts rejecting it in various ways, depending on other factors.

Like all the major errors of our time, this one has created an epidemic, because we all refuse to see that illnesses are imbalances created by mind, not punishments from an arbitrary god or fate.

Heart disease, another main feature of our culture, is closely related to diabetes, in that it shares features of dysfunctional love, painful, controlling love, a love we think we have a right to expect and own. We can either treat a heart problem and diabetes separately, or we can find the emotions at the bottom of both and free them up...

Because medicine cannot quantify emotion and belief, the patient is never pointed into the direction of self-healing by a doctor, which makes it nearly impossible for a diabetic to find to a cure. The diabetic needs to become aware of his response to cultural processes and then de-program herself from what does not work for her and also—stay away from sugar and Tanduay.

To be falsely sweet and loving is the major mistake that catches us particularly at Christmas time! It always turns sour when the guests leave and the sweets are eaten, the sweet smiles spent.

Aiming at a cure, the diabetic needs to be honest and truthful in matters of love and she needs to give up the notion that love is a "feeling" you receive from others. Love is not that!

Love is complete giving, not planning to receive back. Love is to look after family happily, not from duty, guilt, religious or cultural reasons we don't dare question.

Love is not needing to feed your children sweets because you can give them the real thing...

This kind of honesty, in conjunction with eating real food, will keep the diabetic from eating "emotional sugar" and end the reason for her to be ill.

She needs to understand that her illness comes from how she relates to love and how to balance love to become a nurturing force.

This will also address the heart disease that so often goes with diabetes for those same reasons.

"Insulin" is a chemist's word for the ability to assimilate love. You can either inject it every day or teach your body to produce it sufficiently... To manage symptoms with insulin does not deal with the underlying cause and should be no more than emergency medicine.

The best magic given by nature for adjusting sugar levels is to smell that sour poop before it sinks! When the body finds out how exactly digestion has gone wrong, it will adjust, without you even thinking about it. Smelling sugar turned sour also kills the appetite for more sugar! Even drinking a mouthful of vinegar will spoil the taste of a cake or sugary shake, just like a sour hang-over puts us off alcohol for a while.

Our individual kind of sour smell, which is our own bodies' response to mal-digested sugar, has immense value as a bio-feedback for us! It helps us face our own *good feelings turned sour* and the exact reasons for that. The correction here is direct and immediate, and only gradually becomes conscious later.

My lungs still full of sour love... I leave the shithouse, smiling at the washing women, and go back into the restaurant. I cancel my order of mango-milkshake and pancakes—then proceed to the local eatery and get fish, rice and bananas.

The cook smiles at me and I smile back. No cake needed.

Chapter 6: Rancid man

You have met him, a good few times in your life! And there was no need to smell out his shit before you steered hard past his outstretched hand, shocked to the core by his body odour, and keeping your breath in until you were well out of reach, diplomacy be damned.

You know what I mean?

I met him on Hikkaduwa beach, Sri Lanka, where he seemed a nice guy, so freshly washed and eating fruit. Not so much bad breath either.

Later, he spent a night at our place after having a good night meal together. The next morning (it was 1 pm), when I tried to awaken the big, snoring man, I nearly died upon entering his room! It smelled like a dozen old, rotting corpses, all stacked up there for the last few months, and I had to breathe this decay for minutes, so hard was he to shake back into life! Later, the bed and blanket had to be moved outside for sunning, the room disinfected with a bottle of sandalwood essential oil and his forgotten socks incinerated behind the house...

Imagine a dead fox in his hole and you putting your head in to sniff him out...

No, I never followed him to the toilet, although I do remember fatty smears, when I finally visited that part of the house again.

This guy proved to be, underneath all his "coolness," full of unacknowledged fears. He completely suppressed anger, sadness and self-doubt behind a smile and a clever word.

You could talk with him about feelings, which was interesting to him, but he would not live some of those at all, not act upon them, and not trust them to influence a decision.

I met a few rancid people of that calibre in my life. Their shit is glossy, whether it is formless or a well-shaped sausage. The oily surface of those sausages makes them easy sliders in the large intestine and sticky ones in a porcelain toilet. You need to brush. Do it sooner rather than later...

Some people claim that foul smells are the worst, but at least they smell kind of fertile...

Rancid smell is the smell of unholy death, at least to most noses! It speaks, or rather does not speak of things felt a long time ago, that have died and been left unburied. There is the stagnant waft of slow airless decay, mummifying the acrid sharpness underneath.

May be this is why we so avoid the rancid man, or is it his personality, only introduced by this odour of rotting fat...?

Causalities are usually reversible in nature, as all things interconnect, and thus the smell of a person always describes the person who produces that smell. Any dog knows that.

Then what is it that a dog reads out of the smell of rancid man?

A little like cat—fed on corned beef...

A little like the terribly sad and fearful pig he has eaten...

And like a man who would eat such food and who would also feed fatty foods to his cat.

Dog smells quite easily the fearful rejection of emotional self, sees through the cover...

Why does rancid man not digest feelings he craves to seek out? Well, it is not that unusual to seek what we can't have, including feelings we lost a long time ago.

My main rancid man was once a scared little boy who had to disconnect from living his unrequited love for uninterested, neglectful parents. His love was suffocated but never forgotten or let go. He believed in friendship, love, trust, loyalty, but could not live these values himself, not in his practical heart. He rather lived the lack of these feelings or the phantoms of those old and mummified ones, he could not resurrect...

Rancid man likes open people, but cannot open up himself, not even to himself. He can be quite fearful, but carefully acts casual, keeping his fears, self-doubts and true emotions a well-guarded secret.

He clings to how his emotions were first experienced and is too scared to try again. Not for real.

One could think, when looking at a body, that *muscle rises to the challenge*, while *fat is a coward*, avoiding all action. This view however misleads us into thinking of fat as generally "bad," which may be fashionable, but is in fact quite incorrect. Fat as such is not the problem! Any man looking at a set of great boobs knows that.

Fat can be, and is in essence, the agent of lubrication, facilitating all movement and action!

The deciding factor between fat being "good" or "bad" is therefore whether it is used for the lubrication of physical, mental and emotional processes, or left unused, deposited to rot, by a stagnant, scared and disconnected personality.

Fat can be "good" and "bad" in many ways. In a cold climate, animal fat is the main asset for surviving the winter. In a tropical climate, the same fat would just fatten people up or turn rancid, as they cannot make use of it.

Here comes the European tourist out of his winter to tropical Thailand, continues eating pork as before and wham—his heart aches, he gains weight, sweats a lot, his cholesterol goes roof—and his shit turns rancid. Eventually it turns liquid, since pork and chickens host many times more salmonella than he is used to from home.

The Inuit on the other hand can live almost exclusively on fats, as he digests it well in his cold climate and because he lives and feels deeply all there is, and without distortions.

The other main external discernment about fat has to be its quality. Fat does not equal fat, not in the body and not in your food! In fact, there is hardly a more desirable food than avocado oil or sesame and olive oil, which are embraced by the body and digested easily.

These oils are great medicine and absolutely essential to good health! I love adding these oils to my salads. Makes me feel so good...

I also eat a lot of oily fish, which is my personal health insurance and serves to produce great "shit-cakes."

On the other side, there is fat that deserves the name "shit" more than the term "food!"

There is the depressed pig in its cage, killed after pumping itself up with the fear of death! Its fat is full of antibiotics, growth hormones, oestrogen, adrenaline, fear, dullness and unhappiness and that is then what we eat with our daily cutlet...

This is not food suited for humans or dogs and no body will tolerate it for long without rejecting it in one of various ways.

Normally, we just don't like the taste of bad fats or old ones near rancidity—and don't eat them. Or we throw them back up.

Rancid man however often cannot tell the difference between old and new feelings or between fats he can handle and the ones he can't. He may eat such pork and fry-ups unexamined, as he gorges on feelings he does not examine.

If you want to meet rancid man, you best watch those tourists arriving in the tropics from their winter, spending their days stoned around the main beach restaurant, indulging in the "munchies!" They will eat more, more indiscriminately and more emotionally, after getting "high," and their individual psychosis will tend to be more activated, telling them to feel even better by eating those "feely" foods, like sugar and fat!

Power plants are meant for shamans, not for the general public out for a "buzz!" If you don't listen to their signs and signals and just continue being a consumer, eating for fun, they work against you and they will decrease your ability to digest the unnecessary foods you eat. The ph. in your mouth changes, you have less saliva and less digestive juices in the stomach.

Those who ask for increased feeling and experience by taking drugs, do usually just what rancid man does—asking for more emotion than they can handle! This similarity of psychological profile means that many rancid people you meet will also be drug users, craving eternally for more—and making no use of it.

Using actual, that is man-made, drugs of any kind, always influences digestion and will change your shit into something very different. Any reading of character or emotional imbalance becomes then quite difficult and the physiological imbalances shown are usually taken as a result of that drug.

Rancid man always has his reasons for why he won't let fresh air touch those deepest, secret feelings he won't admit to. He might be a thief, a secret agent or an under-cover cop, who cannot live what he truly feels, and she might be a rancid lady holding on to ancient feelings or to lovers she can't let go. They both need fresh air!

Children don't seem to get rancid smells, which require years to develop. They are still in touch with original feeling.

But rancid man does not feel loved, nor does he like himself deep down. It would be very therapeutic for him to fall in love, but no sentient female wants to be close to him! He hides this even from himself.

What can he do? He can cut out all bad fats from his diet for good. But he should start with a meditation on smelling his rancid shit for twenty minutes as a bio-feedback! Then do a bowel cleanse. The Yoga-technique of "Shank Prakshalana" will cleanse the bowel-walls completely, while the squeamish can eat psyllum husks. He then fasts on apples and carrots for one to two weeks before proceeding with a fruit and vegetable-based diet. This being very difficult for him psychologically, he needs to regain the emotional content he has substituted for by eating fat, or else submit to his craving. It is very important to smell every stool produced during this process and to gradually take those emotional contents back out of the digestion and back into full personal ownership.

Meditating on those lost feelings, while fasting and shitting, is the most direct path. Honesty with self and openness with others are the windows he must open to let out this smell of rancid decay he has been holding inside himself.

Staying away from drugs and alcohol completely, eating raw parsley and running in the forest every day will strengthen the rancid man.

His main task is then to throw out those old emotions and find the courage to become empty enough for fresh ones.

Just remember, dear reader—If you ever invite rancid man into your home—feed him nothing but apples, keep the windows open and—don't inhale those forgotten socks!

Chapter 7: Blood and piles

Many years ago, I found myself in an out-of-the-way place on Guadeloupe, West Indies.

I had a fever and couldn't get around for some fruit and water. There was however a little house and an old lady I asked for food and water. She had little water, as a hurricane had polluted the supply, but showed me a packet of pasta. "Spaghetti!" Yes, I nodded. But what I then got was the boiled pasta on a plate with some ketchup, no oil, nothing. Stupidly, I ate it all, drank my mouthful of water and went back to being feverish...

The next day I took a boat to the little island of Terre-de-Haut, where I camped on the far and unpopulated side.

I tried to have my regular morning dump—but nothing.

Three days later, I still couldn't shit and was getting too uncomfortable to wait another day. So I decided to get it done no matter what and began to really try to force it out with intermittent yoga and hard squeezing. Nothing!

The next day I felt awfully ill and there was no way to reach a doctor or even a shop for some oil. It *had* to come out...so I slipped two fingers into my arse to get the toughest first bit out manually... My fingers touched solid concrete! I scratched off little bits that proved to be as hard as stone, but couldn't move the main cork. By that time, blood was trickling down my legs, squatting there in the bushes and I was sweating like on my very last leg...

I had a fleeting sympathy for menstruating women, which soon became the horror of a mother giving birth to a twelve-pound baby in the wilderness...

To cut a very long and painful story blissfully short, I ended up with my entire hand up my arse, breaking off rock after little rock, while standing in a quickly gathering pool of blood, trying not to faint before

I was finished…This was the day when I would have valued a bottle of coconut oil over a bottle of the world's most expensive champagne…

Obviously, since this experience I have always owned an enema-squeezer and avoided meticulously to get mentally or physically constipated, especially when travelling on the trodden path.

Not many are quite that stupid as to combine plain pasta with no drinking, fever and the necessary "control" of getting to a new place. But most tourists go down this trail to a good degree, when they first travel to a new country, especially a tropical place! They eat pasta and fries, instead of rice; they don't drink enough water, but lots of dehydrating beer; the temperatures give them a slight fever. And then there are the psychological mistakes…

What is really—a traveller? A traveller is a person who has left family, friends and all familiar ground behind, including her language, culture and daily habits and now has to adapt to a completely different *outside*! She has had to let go of her past identity, the comfortable and familiar and her old view of self, reinventing herself in response to ever-changing new impressions and experiences. At least that is what she ought to do in order to stay in balance…

A traveller is usually also a person who receives far more impressions than she gives expressions!

What comes from the *outside* into our minds—the total of our impressions—can easily multiply by a factor of a hundred! When you sit in a train from Bangkok to Chiang Mai, you can watch half of Thailand floating past your tired eyes in only twelve hours. How does that compare with seeing the same, repetitive daily images in your office, where you could work blind-folded?

Or walk through the big market in Mazatlan, Mexico, where your eyes fall shut after an hour of seeing so many colours, so many interesting details, that you just can't digest any more…

The "input" of exotic travel to the traveller's mind is phenomenal. But what about "output?" What about expressing, giving of self, letting go trustingly and thus giving back experience?

The old-hand traveller does just that. He will not change places every few days, only every few months. He stays for the rainy season in a village, where he teaches the kids some useful stuff, helps out with fishing, improves people's English and tells stories of far-away countries.

He *gives back*, as if he was still with his family at home. He gives what he is, sleeps in shared huts and trusts local food. He does not hide behind divisions and resort fences and does in this way not get out of balance between "receiving" and "giving," impressions and expressions!

He also eats less for the first few days, while his body/mind adjusts to temperature, people, food and bacteria, and he stays low key with alcohol. Eating bananas, papaya, lychees and other peel-able fruit for the first couple of days prevents most digestive disorders later by giving the system time to adjust.

He said good-bye to his friends and to yesterday. He is here now and adapts without resistance.

The budding young traveller from England on the other hand, will get really drunk on his first day in Bangkok, try every-thing exotic he comes across and "'ave a nostalgic steak and fries for dinner to feel at 'ome." He continues consuming, as he did in England, but now he is in "holiday mode," mainly nourished by beer, staying in his resort bar where he learns to see the locals as waiters or prostitutes. He buys everything he desires (holiday!) and gives nothing back (worked all year for this shit!). He "deserves" his two weeks holiday a year, "fer Christ sake."

Does it surprise, that he cannot shit for days, when he "takes it all in" while giving nothing back? You may try telling him—but he doesn't "give a shit."

An attitude of "holding on" or "having it all," rather than to equally give, and to let go mentally and emotionally, must always affect the body and digestion because of their fundamental oneness and fine balance! You need to *digest* all of your many experiences emotionally, while at the same time digesting your food (TV is much like travel there!) and one will always affect the other.

But it goes deeper than that. There is a reason behind how the English guy acts in Bangkok! The reason is that this bohemian fellow is actually quite scared about being alone in the big wide world! After reading of all the dangers in his tourist guide—malaria, earth quakes, hurricanes, bacteria, rip-off agents, taxis, un-washed tomatoes—he does not really trust those easy smiles on those brown, slit-eyed faces, nor does he trust the water or the food he eats...He just eats it for comfort, to assure himself that all is okay, that he is safe and that nothing much has changed...

He seeks out the company of his compatriots for that same reason, which requires even more beer, until he finally falls asleep despite the heat in a room he has not yet seen and despite the roaring music. He forgets to drink his glass of water...

English tourists nearly all come in this pattern. You can predict at the airport, that in five days' time they will be constipated and lobstered...I call this phase one.

The way to deal with those fears that everybody has before travel is to acknowledge and face them! Not many people can do this of course and find countless mechanisms to avoid or control their fears. This brings them out of their bodies and into the head, where they centre themselves at the expense of their digestion.

The finding a new ability to flow with the present is not helped but only replaced by drinking beer. There is no adaptation of the awareness to the new environment, no adaptation of the digestive organs to new food, not even a good-bye to what was real yesterday...

Such a tourist expects everything to be the same as at home—the moves of calling waiters, her fries, the toilet and the way she talks to people. She does not take the risk to visit a remote village without "amenities," would not accept an invitation to eat dog or iguana with the local family, and she has taken out an inclusive travel insurance policy.

Deep down she has turned into a fearful control freak in denial, but she hides it behind that confident smile of the one who "made it to Thailand."

Not admitting to those travel-fears stops us from *flowing* and gets us constipated, particularly when this denial leads us to do things that accelerate its effect.

I've seen this hundreds of times, always in the same basic pattern...One could make a living from keeping a bottle of coconut oil and little enema syringes at hand, when the newest arrivals from London start ordering opulent meals and beer...

They tend to think me psychic for knowing all about their toilet-troubles the following days, unaware of how obvious it really is...

If shitting were fully legal and commonly accepted as real, tourist offices might give out pamphlets on the real dangers, given that bad shitting is the number one cause for a holiday "turned to shit ..."

The constipated character becomes instantly manifest in the traveller, but it is the one who stayed home, too scared of such change, who is the hardest and densest shitter.

Successful control-freaks are chronically constipated. Those who lose that control regularly, alternate between bouts of pebbles and bouts of mud. Both produce high toxicity-levels and instability in their bowels, which makes them increasingly vulnerable to the high population density of tropical bacteria. Long term they face gout, arthritis, haemorrhoids and even bowel cancer.

Controllers often develop haemorrhoids, brought forth by regular hard pushing, which can make their holidays a bloody affair. These piles are nearly impossible to cure and most might like to prevent constipation in the first place, rather than vainly stuffing shark fat, horse chestnut depositories and frozen sticks up their arses. None of these things work even a little, nor is burning or cutting piles very successful. A St. John's-wort oil enema after shitting manages the symptoms to a degree. Eating papaya and walking help, but it takes years of un-constipated work to get over chronic piles. Giving birth and lifting weight brings them on as well and should be avoided by pebble-people.

Chronic hard shit cannot be cured just by eating fruit and raw vegetables alone. It is highly psychological and goes along with all kinds of controlling behaviour. A European woman travelling through Sumatra on her own, feeling like a sexual "target," will likely constipate, as will misers on a budget. And if you don't trust the water, you may not shit at all...

It all starts in the plane, of course. Eating normal amounts, while you cannot move or breathe fresh air, brings on your first pebbles. So, eat apples on the plane and skip the free "meals."

Sexual inhibitions also constipate chronically! It is real fun when you're out fishing for the day, with a few people in a little boat, and they start needing to do *it*! Folk without sexual inhibitions or anal psychosis will just hang their arses over board and go for it... But most "civilized" contemporaries won't even dare contemplate such a possibility, nor do they have the physical skill! So they try to make you go back home to the toilet bowl, to which I never submit before sunset or deteriorating weather... Remain the options of pooping into the bailing jar or going for a swim. This is where I tell the ladies about those mako sharks we have here in the Bay of Islands...it is so much fun! And better than Gestalt-therapy!

You can either get over your privacy issues in a boat and let go—or get sea-sick and badly constipated, especially after a hot, sunny day.

It is okay to shit from a dinghy though and it can even transform an odd catholic hang-up around sexuality into a useful burley-trail!

Letting go of what controls us most will help with hard shit and so does *giving* in all its forms. An attitude of relaxed, grateful giving is what is needed most!

Meditate on that rather than on the newspaper—and give the world freely all that is inside you, without hesitation or reservation!

Don't use European toilet seats, if you can help it! Squat in a low Tai Chi–stance and let go of your shit consciously. The tension in your thighs makes your gut-movements much stronger! Then give! Afterwards feel the pebbles with your fingers to know how hard they are, smell them, see the darkness of their colour—and finally feed them to some outdoor plant!

Be proud of what you gave back! Promise some to the plants watching...

Add to this a shoulder-stand to bring the blood back out of your piles.

Be giving and open throughout your day. Let go!

And if you're about to give birth—please read this chapter again! You'll need it!

Remember—there is light at the end of every tunnel!

Chapter 8: The Running Man

The paper-roll holder squeals like a Shimano fishing reel, a kingfish tearing out the line!

(Lots of trees must die each year for the Running Man...)

Another scream of the reel announces recognition of a wet mess from splash-back, over thighs, balls and buttocks...this is a serious case!

Silly of him to use a seated toilet, when fifty meters away he could have used an Asian drop, where his balls would have been safe, his thighs clean, his anus washable, and the windows already open... Instead he now needs a shower or a wiping of those dripping balls with more dead trees...

Just as I had surmised—there's more bubbly wet splashing, and another kingfish takes off...a brackish fragrance hovers over the acoustics and wafts about lessons not learned and a world bought but not quite entered. I call this phase two.

The most popular of all travel ailments is undoubtedly having the shits! You can get them straight away, of course, but most commonly travellers start with being scared and controlled and constipated for the first few days and then reach a tipping point, where the body needs to finally rid itself off the accumulated toxins in the gut. Constipation makes very vulnerable towards bacteria as it weakens immunity considerably, and direct sunlight speeds up this process even further. At this stage, the traveller eats something unusual or too much and—bang—he starts vomiting and shitting like a fish! To try and stop this natural process with charcoal or chemistry just paralyses the gut further and is a grave error. No—vomiting and shitting is the cure! Unless it goes on and on...

You can indeed watch them running between bars and toilets, even learning the Tagalog words for "shithouse" and "toilet-paper," much to the quiet amusement of the helpful locals!

The "Running Man" is well known on tropical beaches and he is famous for blaming it all on bacteria and local food. He has lost the control he has been clinging too, now feeling the fear he has suppressed, and he wonders just how sick he might get. Is there a doctor he can trust? Could this be cholera, or typhus or food poisoning or worse...?

The Running Man is flowing with his fears now and ready to *give*. He wants to tell his fellows about how sick he feels and he lets go of some pretences at this stage. It is good that he lets go, but does he find back into a balance?

Running Man often keeps running, unable to accept this new reality or the food or his fears. A two-week tourist simply won't consider staying off the restaurant food for a few days to allow his bowels to settle! He wants to make "the most" of his holiday and continues boozing and eating and motor-biking as usual, ruining his digestion completely. He runs for two weeks and gets severe head-aches from dehydration, before finally leaving this "shitty country" and its "bad food" behind for good.

The Running Man is the source of reports on lack of hygiene and lack of care in food preparation in countries like Thailand, Philippines or Mexico. He never *owns* his own inability to hold and digest new emotion and new food. The "shits" have nothing to do with his attitudes of course, only with "bacteria," even though he sees the locals and the real traveller enjoying that same food without any complaint!

His doctor helps him with blaming the poor bacteria and without fail suggests chemical control.

The Running Man does of course not just *run* to the shithouse. He ran from the "shit" of his work routine and from the cultural confines of his country, from "taking shit" from his boss, and from commitments—just to get here...Now he still runs from place to place, country to country, beach to beach. He cannot be content with what he has and where he is, nor can he appreciate the present. It is all about the next town, the next bus, the future and about "having it all" at once.

If he does not travel, the Running Man is a business executive or any engaged participant in the "rat-race," whose main orientation is that of "success," of "making it," and of running after things all day, that have nothing or very little to do with who he is, what his needs are, or what he can emotionally digest.

Just as *holding on to the past* slows down peristaltic movement, so does *living in the future* speed it up! If you strive to achieve "success" instead of enjoying the process here now, you will start running, and if you do that every day—you become the Running Man.

In the western world, the Running Man is the most common character, even though the fibre-less food we eat hides the symptoms to a large degree. It is the thinker and the head-centred person who is likely to start running and the faster and the more superficial his thoughts are, the more he runs.

If you run from thought to thought in the office, you will have a much more nervous digestion than if you make your living from a little fishing boat catching fish on a hand-line...

"Thinking" therefore does not help the Running Man, nor does "doing." What he needs is to accept being here now, to relax with *what is* and to simply *be*! Forget yesterday, tomorrow, travel plans, planes and internet cafes, and be here for real!

Internet cafes are very bad for digestion! They are full of those who haven't let go of the past and of those who are already "back" in the future...

Constipated tourists read their mail every day and keep thinking deeply about the past, without writing much, while the "runners" write about what they will do, once they're back home. Both patterns worsen the underlying condition of avoidance of their unknown new self here in the present.

Cars, buses, motorbikes and planes are not something the Running Man should think about, as they speed things up that normally move much slower in nature. Instead, he needs to walk slowly or even sit quietly, content with where he is...

He will not learn any of those things his body keeps suggesting if he seeks external or chemical solutions. I sometimes wonder therefore, if it isn't better to let nature work her shit- magic until he is ready to learn, instead of offering early help...

There is however a wonderful trick that in the short term so effectively cures the shitting and vomiting guy, that it always makes me the "famous healer" to the entire beach!—I give the Running Man fresh, strong ginger tea on empty stomach and get him to stick with just that for six hours, doing nothing but *being there*. It always, always works!

And it is a cure-all on the beach, that grounds those with head-aches, fixes the sleepless when taken with honey, and generally tones immunity and digestion.

It is easy to make a living on such beaches from always having ginger handy...it is regularly the first thing I check out on a new island, after seeing where I'd go in a typhoon and where I get the beach-herb against jelly-fish stings...

Ginger fixes the Running Man, but he should not be tempted to see the "runs" as just a haphazard or "negative" thing to rid himself of and forget! If he does not face his shit, smell it and own it, he will always retain the Running Man potential, for the rest of his life!

By smelling and even touching his watery mess, the Running Man can come fully into the present, into his true inner reality. Then he can quit running inside, because reality is all he was running from...

One such meditation will probably stop his runs and a good few will end the tendency.

With awareness, it becomes a matter of choice to stop running. We can decide to stop running from things and after things!

There is nothing wrong with being a business executive or with being competitive. But we need to balance that out, not run with it on all channels all of the time, deep into our private lives and over meal-times!

We can learn to hold and behold in appreciation what we have at our hands already, and be content.

We can learn to accept the emptiness after vomiting and shitting, the emptiness we so fear, and use it to pursue that specific self-knowledge which overcomes the disposition.

If we got the guts!

Certainly, some adjustment to a common-sense diet is necessary, specifically during and after the bout. It is important to avoid sugar and stir-fries, anything fried in oil.

After a day's fast, the Running Man should eat boiled rice, bananas and fish, if he is hungry, but only a little.

The best insurance is to keep having that cup of ginger tea (no tea-bags!), but the cure is always in the mind that needs to make a shift.

Don't feel sorry for yourself! Self-pity is a victim's method to stay ill and stagnant!

Find a positive way to enjoy yourself, instead of focusing on what you don't like.

Don't make people hate you by joining them on island-hopping dive trips while you're on the 'run'!

You can however go for a swim, where there are no people and lots of fish, just before you need to take the next shit! It is an amazing experience! Tropical, colourful fish in their thousands, all around you eating your shit! Trust your snorkel and watch yourself surrounded by all these many fish you are feeding, which will even save the trees by eating clean your very arse...

This is a delightful adventure the hard shitter can only dream of and the Running Man alone can enjoy!

The trick to travelling is to not move around on a constant search for more to see, but go to a tropical, beautiful place and really behold and enjoy that place, its little joys, its people, its food, with the content appreciation that all you ever needed is here now already.

Chapter 9: Empty yourself!

How can we have our cup of life filled with golden wine, when all we have now is a cup full of dirty water?

Is this not the wail at the root of our daily song?

A question so difficult to answer though, that few can claim to have arrived at the solution! Gandhi probably, Osiris, Buddha...

Oh, we try! We filter and sieve and disinfect, to get the impurities out of the water. Our science claims it can make drinking water out of dish-water! The old alchemists and Jesus might even have changed it into wine and we can almost do that too.

It just takes far longer than the thirsty man can wait...

Even with the new age of spiritual seeking only a very, very few experience this filling of their cup with golden wine and are instead content with magic powders and accounts of strangers who might or might not have had such an experience.

We sing and fiddle over it, quite unready for any major or fundamental change in our thinking and our world-view.

We're fishing for higher truth in a pool of dirty water and while we make the water dirtier still, this truth escapes and gradually becomes a mystery.

Knowledge as we know it, is a "doctoring around," a gradual amassing of preconceptions that are only consistent with each other, but not with *what is* beyond our cultural perspectives. History shows that science moves from old misconceptions to more modern misconceptions, from theory to theory, without ever getting closer to existential truth.

Everything we believed yesterday we know for wrong today. And all we believe today, they're going to find hilarious tomorrow...

This type of "knowledge" is what we gather or have others gather for us, and after some time we "know" so much, we think ourselves "educated." At this stage, our pride ends all real further enquiry...

In reality, we are filled up with second-hand beliefs and cultural definitions, with our parents' fallacies and with divisive religious fairy-tales, to the rim! We worry about "cults," but it is our society itself which insists to be the omnipotent and exclusive cult, telling us precisely what to think, how to think, how to feel, what to want, or else...

Are we not all completely brainwashed by our cultures to like rugby or baseball or to dislike eating insects? Do we not buy notions like "just war" and "defence of democratic freedom" as readily as the mullahs talk about "holy war"—depending on which program runs our brain? Are we not Christians only because our parents are? Do we not pray to Allah simply because we are born in a particular country? Our beliefs are based on geography and political religion, not on enquiry!

The mental content which amounts to our view of the world and of ourselves is all unverified and unexamined programming that we have received since we were born.

We are filled up with illusions that replace our self-responsibility, our instincts, our autonomy and the simplicity of perceiving what is real.

No matter how hard we may try—It would take us a million years to filter and sieve and repair and add to our assumptions and errors to a point where we achieve the clarity necessary to perceive reality as it is.

But there is a solution! The simplest of all solutions...

Take your cup of life, with all its definitions of who you are and what the universe is supposed to be. Lift up that cup with all that false "knowledge," your schooling, your cultural, religious, parental and scientific beliefs and—empty it!

To empty the cup is the only path possible, if we want to ready ourselves to receive the profoundly new and ultimately the divine.

The only way that actually works...

As a traveller, you quickly find out that you can't add new shit to old shit, when adapting to a different culture or to a tribal community that puts your world-view upside down!

You can't learn the new language as long as you think in your old one and you can't understand a culture of head-hunters, of sexual rites of passage or of ancestor worship, without first dropping your own cultural prejudices and definitions around death and sex.

Unless you get over your cultural understanding of death as the opposite of life and as an eternal nothingness or hell, you cannot help but look at such a culture through the blind glasses of your own narrow horizon—and see it as "superstitious" and ignorant.

Even the anthropologist cannot perceive the reality of these people with any more clarity than his own "fullness" or his "knowledge" allow. He can never comprehend a shamanic ritual unless he drops his limiting western ideas on reality and his academic arrogance.

When you travel South-East Asia for six months or so, you leave behind your family and friends, your language and culture, the food you know, the toilet to sit on.

You don't just add a nice little travel experience to your normal life, as you would in a three-week holiday, but instead empty yourself of the world as you know it and of your cultural definitions! When you don't speak English for a few months, you see your language from the outside, your culture from the outside—and the old programs become obvious as such...That is when you start dropping them!

You start emptying yourself of your definitions of who you are and what life supposedly is.

The more easily and completely you let it all go, the easier it becomes to learn those Kampuchean words, to digest the food of mountain tribes (lizards and shit...), and to meet the real people! And to come out of our head to start communicating on non-mental levels, as those peoples do...

It is all about emptying out who we thought we were...

It takes a real traveller's courage and a little faith!

The same thing is true about trying to find God!

We can't find God for one simple reason—she is not hiding!

Nor is God anything alike what we are looking for, what we define as "God," what we know or believe about God. So we don't see God. Like fish are unable to know water...

The God of our cultural definition is nowhere in sight! So "he" becomes a "mystical" or "mysterious" "force," that either lives above the clouds, or beyond death, or in any other reality, but never here, now, in sight, in touch...

If we can drop entirely our man with the white beard, the "mystical force" and the "white light" and all our various concepts and supposed bits of knowledge about God—we can become naturally aware of *what is*! And when you live a while with what is—you recognize *its* divinity...but early is this talk about wine.

Back to shit. It is quite impossible to see the truth beyond all our concepts while hanging on to those old concepts of reality, of God and of the human condition that our cultures have conditioned us to make our own. This shit needs to be dropped!

In order to perceive that deepest truth, which we may call God or "bliss," or whatever, we first need to become empty! Empty of all our beliefs, of our parents' beliefs, our cultural beliefs. Our beliefs as a species...

Empty of national or personal pride! Empty of greed! Empty of our anger and of our loneliness, empty of our jealousy. Empty of hypocrisy. Empty.

The path towards truth that actually works is to see, admit, and drop our illusions!

Basically, we are far too full of shit to perceive anything beyond our beliefs and expectations and the other mirror-reflections of our so particular way of looking at reality. We need to recognize our science and beliefs as cultural and arbitrary, in order to free ourselves from their absolute influence and find out what we ourselves perceive, when we look with clarity at is-ness.

You can never experience God while keeping your present view of reality. You need to empty yourself completely—as in vomiting and shitting, sometimes crying!

Neither can we find daily happiness without emptying out our anger, our fear of death, our greed and our arrogance first. Any attempt to be happy through money, success, lovers or positive affirmations is futile, unless we drop the need for money, success and the avoidance of what we have defined as "negative."

All spiritual and worldly progress starts therefore with looking at your shit honestly and in detail. Not analyse! Just look!

Only the awareness of what is illusion and falseness can enable us to empty that cup we would have filled with glorious wine! Trying to be "positive" while all our shit is still inside us can only lead to more constipating illusions, never to fresh insight.

Self-development has to begin with emptying that cup of "knowledge." One has to embrace emptiness!

And here is the problem—as consumers we see emptiness as the antithesis to our most fundamental emotional paradigm! We love to fill ourselves up with food, with experience, other people's beliefs and fashionable delusions, with drugs and with religious and scientific fantasy! Being "full" is to us like feeling rich and safe, while emptiness reminds us of poverty, death and non-being...

Consumers abhor being empty and avoid it like the devil!

And to look at their own "shit?" That is the hardest thing of all...Even the suggestion is offensive.

Even supposedly "advanced" people, and particularly the proud and educated, become instantly defensive when others point at their "shit," even though this is the fastest way to learn! They resent the implication of their own fallibility!!

Very, very few people are ever grateful for criticism ...

They talk about "unconditional love," before they even try to discover all their *conditions.* They "develop" higher chakras, before getting the first one, the arse, sorted and they talk about the "divine light," before having walked their own shadows...

I met hundreds of seekers on my travels, some sadhus, and a few gurus, and found that underneath their blissful smiles they mostly still adhere to either their old concepts or to new ones! Only once have I met a true master who was completely empty of all illusion and division and who I trusted could shit the perfect sausage ...

This man was empty of all concepts and thus effortlessly made me see how full of shit I was in contrast.

Balances in nature are absolute. Fullness and emptiness are the two sides of the same coin, no matter what we may prefer, just like a block of steel is both full and also empty space, when we look closely enough. If we prefer fullness over emptiness, as we all do, the emptiness does not just disappear. It goes underground! After a while we feel emotionally empty, empty of purpose and alone with all we have and with what we stuff ourselves with. The body starts vomiting and shitting then, to bring the emptiness back where it belongs and tries to cure us from being too full of ourselves. Just like a fast, shitting is the agent of emptiness that offers us a chance to correct our imbalances! Fasting, vomiting and shitting reduce our mental "shit" to a point, where we have a chance to find out who we really are when we are not busy filling the inner void.

The idea is to shit consciously, to vomit without resistance and to fast not to lose weight, but to meditate on being empty. This is the cure for excessive fullness!

It can be a truly religious experience to vomit after eating peyote and then stare at what we brought up! It makes us aware of every impurity we ever felt and it shrinks our illusions considerably, as many Native Americans well know. Shitting can be like that too!

While fasting is culturally at least somewhat acceptable, vomiting and shitting are not and have therefore not become "classical" meditation techniques. No guru talks about shitting!

And yet—conscious shitting is the real answer to our unconscious eating, to the obesity epidemic and to seeing the truth on the other side of our self-imposed walls.

So take a full look at the agent of your "dark side" before you flush, and be gratefully aware of all the shit you are giving up. Then empty that bowl, let your shit go, and enjoy the loss!

Enjoy the absence of thought, the stillness that comes with this moment of emptiness.

Your body is now like the empty cup, and if you're quite conscious of that—so is your mind.

Chapter 10: Bullshit

When we fail to empty out the mental and emotional "shit" that continues to press us, this shit needs to express itself somehow. To avoid facing our smelliest parts of ourselves, we suppress and "disinfect" it as much as we possibly can, which always eventually leads to mental and physical symptoms. Usually, we invent moral cultural rules to collectively avoid the "shit" we try to hide from the most, that which scares us "shitless."

But every force provokes an equal and opposite counter-force and therefore all things we suppress tend to jump back up, and into such areas of our lives where we can least control them!

This is divine intelligence at work and evidence that control and suppression do not work.

Apart from body-symptoms the most prominent stage for this suppressed "shit" is our language!

When we look at the English language, we notice that the words "shit" and "fuck" are the most commonly used nouns and verbs of all. Why is this so?

One vital clue is that when we say "shit" and "fuck" we almost never mean to speak of defecation or love-making! We can rather mean a range of blatantly unrelated things, replacing half the language with these two words! There must be over a hundred colloquial idioms made up of shit and fucking...

Why is that so? Why is "shit" and "fuck" eating so deeply into the English language? Well, because the English culture suppresses sexual and anal issues more than anything else and more than other cultures!

The more problematic we find sexuality, the more we force it underground, where it dwells with a will to jump back up, and the more disgusted we feel about some "shit," the more energy this shit" will gather in our subconscious minds.

The English teach their kids not to use the "S-word" (whatever that is), as they are too uncomfortable with sex and shit to factually or respectfully talk about it or even pronounce it.

Such naughty secrets then become highly charged and interesting to all children and they can't stop thinking about it, albeit in distorted ways...

And since they are culturally not allowed to openly talk about things sexual and anal without major embarrassment, this "secret shit" grows and comes out through the skin as pimples and through language—as bullshit!

When a kid comes to be a teenager, and the absolute parental control starts deteriorating, all this suppressed shit wants to come out! This is why teenagers experience acne and this is why they alone modify and change language, not adults.

If we granted children a good relationship with shit and some freedom of natural expression, nobody on earth would replace half the dictionary with "shit" and "fuck!" There would be no motive or energy for such a thing.

Nor would English teenagers have to break out in pimples.

In Australia, where people live relatively close to the slaughter of cows, sheep and "roos," the socially acceptable word "bloody" protects some of Sydney's better society from "fucking up" their lingo too badly. But in the outback, where there are more roos than sheilahs, every third word in their speech is a vari-fucking-ation of the fucking they don't so easily get...

In "good" English society, where the Queen's English suppresses direct language along with body-function, "fucking" and "shitting" have to make do with producing pimples and mental "shit." I imagine that shitting or pissing in public is fined more severely in England than in other places...

While real shitting and fucking as such must not be spoken of or seen by others, the resulting shame and embarrassment keep growing and ever stricter privacy rules become necessary. These rules are now even beginning to threaten publicly breast-feeding mothers...

In native tribes, I have never seen such or any embarrassment, and even in continental Europe it is nowhere as dominant as within the Anglo-Saxon cultural circle.

Eventually, suppressed "shit" gathers enough energy (the energy you constantly employ to hold it down), to become electrically stronger than our conscious thoughts and that is when shit starts rising and eating into our language!

Suppressed truth always fights back! It is very obvious, where we are breeding "terrorists" by suppressing a people to the point of suicide, or attempt to hide a president's sex-life...or tell kids not to swear... Just watch how surely their vows of celibacy drive catholic priests to child-abuse, or consider the piles of corpses of infants and foetuses found under monasteries! The more you suppress things the more they pop up and by suppressing language in vital areas of life, there is a huge chaotic potential for that.

This is how bullshit is created.

Bullshit seems to have nothing to do with actual shit! The "shit" here fills in when we avoid terms like "deceptive," "foolish," "boastful' or "offensive," and the "bull" must mean there is an enormous pile of the wrong stuff! Everyone who has ever tried to milk a bull knows that he is the wrong animal!

The reason why we use fillers for words describing something too truthful and unpopular for civilized taste is that we lack the courage and honesty to openly discuss truth as it presents.

Bullshit serves to avoid calling a spade a spade and finding out what is real and what is not.

We "take shit" and "give shit" back, because what we really take and give must not be examined too closely, lest we become aware of it too much for our own comfort.

When our boss tells us to quit making the same old mistakes we always make—we are "taking shit" from him, since otherwise we'd have to actually look at his criticism and face and own our shortcomings!

When we "give shit" to others, we don't give consideration for how offended they feel and to what exactly we would have them change.

"Giving a shit" or "not giving a shit" is the measure of our love. "I don't care" is for many too much of an admission and to others not quite strong enough to express their utter lack of sympathy. People who "don't give a shit" sound cooler, but are of course chronically constipated mentally and physically, no matter what they eat—while those "shitting" at others all day tend to get the runs, whether there are bacteria present or not (there always are...).

Then they run to the chemist, buying some "shit" to fix it, not having a clue what this "shit" actually is, and what it does. To bother asking would be "chicken-shit" and they of course refuse to be caught "shitting themselves" over such crap...

People who smoke "shit" would often be better off knowing what exactly they smoke and to what purpose. A lack of respect for power-plants and the taking of artificially made drugs can "knock the shit right out of them," or lead to some real "heavy shit."

What beats the shit out of me every time I watch the news, is how little the crap they talk about has anything to do with real life! If you wish to experience top-notch bullshit, you only need to listen to politicians! – "At this stage it would seem inappropriate to make any definitive statements regarding the allegations that this war might have been illegal or unprovoked..." You can listen to this kind of "shit" for hours and not know a real thing afterwards! This is what we might call "institutionalized bullshit," and it pervades every living-room and every mind that lets it in without chewing and properly digesting. This institutionalized bullshit is the life-blood of our democracies today!

While the word "shit" itself is still hypocritically censored out by television and newscast, the remaining cleaned-up content has become such a celebration of "bull" that most television is nothing but shit to real people today.

The biggest pile of "bull" is created by "political correctness," a televised institution that prevents any undesired truth or reality from seeing the light of day. In countries pretending to allow freedom of expression, we find a great need for such non-legal ways to reign in the dissenters and keeping them from saying "offensive" things that go against the messages of the empire! The consumer does rarely wish to realize that the demand to be politically correct is a denial of freedom of expression, and sees of course no parallels to the forced uniformities of the former Soviet Union or the rule of the mullahs...

Isn't it funny how "good society" avoids the truth along with the word shit? A whole body-function has been assigned to the "dark side" and from this underground it keeps eating more and more into our perception of reality...

When we talk about real, actual shit as such, we clinically call it "faeces," "excrement," and "evacuation" to keep the real shit well out of our children's mouths and away from the public nose. On the other hand, "shit" then becomes the universal word, covering and replacing all those other issues we are uncomfortable with, that we can't face and keep secret!

"Shit" has, like a cancer, eaten away word-meanings of all suchness that we perceive as negative, such as in anger, criticism, falseness, boasting, deception, marijuana, hashish, difficulty, rejection. We call all those things "shit" and are done explaining...

We don't want to look at or talk about these "shitty" things any further! We don't want to know the truth about them, so we keep losing more truth to new illusions at every turn.

We kill the words we avoid and thereby transform them into the "shit" we constantly talk and text about. The more shit we transfer like this into the abstract, the more absolute the collective avoidance becomes, until it is firmly structured into rules of morality, into ridiculous laws and finally into cultural "ethics." By then "normal people" are no longer tempted to investigate into the missing pieces, or to question this new "normality," and the few who still do will quickly become ostracized as being deviant or "abnormal." Do we not always say of others what we can't see to be most true of ourselves...?

Once the new cultural reality has been structured into language, the shit is brewing...

Language is the primary programming tool of the mind! Words assign great limitations to suchness for the sake of cultural agreement on what they supposedly mean, and thus limit our individual awareness down to a collective cultural level of dimness.

Language as such comes therefore always with a reduction of awareness. The real important things in life, so we all find, cannot be put into words and they don't fit inside language. But just as blissful silence alone does not teach your kid, so also is a reduction of language or a loss of language equal to a loss of collective awareness...

In other words—If we continue evolution by calling uncomfortable truths "shit," we will, given some time, end up walking around going "shit," "shit," "shit" all bloody day, still knowing what we all mean, and relating better to the consciousness of twitter birds than ever before—but be fuckwits!

How can we heal such a cultural illness? Can we pass a law that makes shit and shitting normal, legal, publicly tolerated, okay to show on TV, okay for children without being yelled at?

You'd have to portray shitting as something "natural" first!!

Imagine we would make shit natural! As in—letting it happen in romantic novels!

Then we could educate our children about shit being good, as all things are that come from inside them. You'd allow them the freedom of expression you might fight wars over—even to express those things with their own mouths that they hear you say in those loaded moments...And you'd not demand from them that they do what you say, but instead live up to the bitter fact that they will only learn from what you do!

You'd teach them, and yourself first, to always mean what you say and you'd teach the truth as a heroic and glorious principle, not as an admission preceding punishment.

You'd then foster the ability to gratefully anticipate and receive criticism as the most bullshit-free form of personal communication. You'd never connect criticism with rejection...Imagine all the people!

Children, who value being given accurate and useful information and advice by honest people, do not need to pull the shit-unloading-trip as teenagers, when they all try to evacuate their parental "bull!"

One of the least recognized of our cultural illnesses is simply that we no longer mean what we say! We dress this up as diplomacy, politeness, self-control, caring, political correctness, sophistication, as cleverness or as "appropriate"—creating an ever-widening gulf between what we say and what we really think and feel to be the truth!

This gulf then also opens between perception and expression and between appearances and factual such-ness...

The division, symbolized by the neck-tie, is lived out in the head as the okay-part of the body and looks down at our bodies as something separate from mind, something we own rather than also are.

"Up" and "down" are to us not the polarity between Heaven and Earth they define, but the location of heaven and hell, of God and the devil! This either/or view we hold costs us half of what in truth is – reality.

One side *is* always "good" and the other side is then "evil!" And who notices how in both "evil" and "devil" we lose half of *life* (reading from the right) –those rejected fifty per cent of reality...

This division is the root-cause of our main cultural imbalances and drives us steadily towards conflict and war.

The possibly most tragic piece of bullshit we produce, buy, and eat every day, and the best example for divisive illusion in our time, would have to be the way we look at "terrorism" and how we see our "war of terror" as the only possible defence of our imagined freedom!

We define a "terrorist" as a person using violence to further her political views on liberty, freedom and survival, and who will kill innocent civilians.

This is what we hate or rather fear about the terrorist.

And what do we ourselves do to further our own political interests of liberty, freedom and survival??

We enact precisely the actions of our supposed "terrorist," by using violence as our sole solution and by killing many, many innocent civilians! We fit of course precisely with our definition of the "terrorist," act precisely like him for the same basic reasons, and we publicly admit capitulation before any philosophy of violence by setting this exact example ourselves!

Like the supposed terrorist, we cannot think of an alternative to violence and we believe that there is only one possible solution, which is to destroy and kill all dissenters and all people housing or hosting them...

We cannot see how our high moral ground exists only on our side of this dividing veil between us and those we see as "others," and that it has of course no validity to the millions of Iraqi and Afghani and Syrian civilians whose families have died in our carpet-bombings!

To them *we* are the real terrorists and they grow up to become freedom-fighters against the "evil" West.

We not only breed terrorism by preempting the "terrorists" and their methods and by being terrorists ourselves, but we actively breed a future generation of new terrorists—kids who now learn from our example and will copy our "war-efforts" and all those vicious methods they see us employ while they grow up! No doubt, that a boy who sees his siblings or parents torn up by American bombs will make a good "terrorist" in the future...

But only sane, undivided people can see that. It is not a matter of opinion or political leaning whether we are for or against such a "war." It is purely a matter of intelligence and of undivided sanity! Our "war on terror" is very much a "war *of* terror" and has all the hallmarks of schizophrenia and megalomania! It leaves no doubt over the degree of our own deep inner divisions...

The only reason why even some supposedly smart people do not see the destruction of democracy and freedom perpetrated by the US worldwide, is the psychological propaganda that creates our cultural division into "us" and "them," into good and evil!

This makes us blind to reality as it presents! We cannot see that killing a hundred thousand Iraqi civilians in the name of "democracy" is terrorism on a large scale, not anything better.

Can it even be accurately called a "war," when an elephant steps on a mouse, or when ten guys beat up on a defenceless child?

How can we attack poor countries illegally and for no reason, without apology to our victims or punishment of the perpetrators as war-criminals—and still think of ourselves as "good," or "just," or "democratic?" How can we replace democracies all over South and Central America with dictatorships of our choice, taking from the poor to feed the rich? That is where overwhelming bullshit kills and destroys the world!

We behave as if it mattered whether Iraq actually had or had wanted weapons of mass destruction or not! But is not the real question how a country that definitely *does* have such weapons and also a history of using them all, should have any right to refuse the same right to arbitrarily selected other countries, simply because they don't belong to their own circle of power? What would we say, if Korea attacked the US for "maybe" having weapons of mass-destruction?? Now that would be insane, despite Korea being quite correct—and we could all see that!

Or - how is it up to us to decide that Israel should be the sole secret atomic power in the Middle-East and that Iran must not do the same, or else? Why do we not treat Israel as we do Iraq for "maybe" possessing nuclear arms? For any just or equitable reasons, do you think?

Why do we condone Israel's threats of unilateral action against Iran - and expect the Iranians to do nothing about it? Because truth and reason are not even part of the equation—only to which side we belong really matters! Where the brainwash comes from!

Israel, being "on our side," can have nuclear arms, but Iraq or Iran, that we consider "others," cannot! We have the military might to say so... And even though the true reasons—oil and US power politics—are rather obvious to a sane mind, westerners instead prefer to believe the bullshit spread by propaganda!

Our twisted perception of reality, the "bullshit" we carry around, does not allow us to realize that we and the "terrorists" of the news are one and the same, and that if we don't like to suffer violence ourselves, we should not employ violence, nor drive people to suicide!

It never seriously occurs to us to end terrorism by looking at the *other* side of our ingrained divisions, and at the worldview of those "others!" We might then listen to their criticism before we hear the blast of a bomb.

It would mean that we'd have to end this nonsense with "good" versus "evil" though, where *we* are always "good" and the *others* always "evil!" We'd then have to be responsible for our own "shit" and drop our massive double standard...

We would have to drop our bullshit...

There are thousands such examples of cultural insanity, wherever we care to look, as our divisions are systemic and omnipresent. Whether we are Christian, Muslim or Jew—all Abrahamic religions lead into that same desert of exclusive either/or and to the mental division between "good and evil," "heaven and hell." They always belong to a "side," fighting holy wars against another such "side ..."

That is why all the wars of our time are started by Jews, Christians and Muslims! They simply won't let go of their basically split reality, or their "hell," for the sake of the good Earth..."Tolerance" for such so-called "religions," that are the exact opposite of "religio," is entirely the wrong attitude! The Abrahamic "religion" is by its nature divisive and violent, and should be treated as the mental illness and the social disaster it is. This would keep most bullshit out of our children's minds for a start!

The same thing happens when we celebrate "Anzac Day" in NZ. Far from having learned our lesson about war, we cultivate as much hero-worship as we possibly can. The silly boys who went to Turkey, killing people they had never even met, because they wanted to prove their manhood, are still proudly sitting in the streets, at ninety, decorated with all their medals, wanting to be honoured for killing! Every passing kid gets the message—a hero is a guy who sheepishly goes to any war around the world, killing people without ever asking why...It is enough for those people we kill to be - *others*!

Even today, we find nothing wrong with killing people in Korea, Vietnam or Afghanistan, as long as England or the rich US lead the way with the right propaganda. We then talk about "defending" our country, even though there was never any attack on it—or dying "for" our country, even though such killing never has benefited our country or any other. This is how rich bullshit can get, and how blind we are when eating it up!

Where "up" is "good," down must be "bad!" So, we like our silly heads—and despise our hairy arses! We like eating, but censor shitting and we only ever like those parts of the truth that flatter our heady egos! And we don't at all mind killing *others*!

We make *others* even of parts of our own bodies! We cut away breasts, stomachs, bellies and long noses with the same violent arrogance, and feel heroic about this too...

We are simply blind to schizophrenia where it is collective, and are no longer capable of perceiving the world as a whole, or at all realistically.

Nothing holds us back like the shit we hold back, and this shit needs to come out as such.

What we need to do as individuals is to reserve saying "shit" to mean only the smelly thing and to call all other things, no matter how uncomfortable that may feel, by their own true names! Why not call "war" the senseless slaughter of civilians that it undoubtedly is? Why not admit that we are far from being "heroes" or "democratic" or even "good?"

Why do we not raise our children to be proud of their being human, rather than "proud to be a Kiwi" or an "American?" Why not keep away from them our religious crap and allow them instead to be truly connected with how things really are?

This alone would help us make it out of the cave and get over the bullshit we're so very, very full of!

Chapter 11: Shit and children

As babies, we have all wanted to play with our shit. We had no problem with it or its smells, unless it was left on our bodies.

We didn't even mind putting it into our mouths at times, if we were able. It wasn't disgusting. Shit was still just shit, without any of the disgust we later learned to associate with it.

Then we saw the horror and stress our parents and other adults showed or hid around us doing our business! Mother would jump up and race through the room to wipe it all away at record speed before we were even done! She jerks us to safety with a yell, when we just tasted it and another day she slaps our fingers for trying to touch it. "Yak!" she goes, pulling her face into a mask of horror...

Then the parents are only happy when you shit into your scary pink potty, thinking it a mortal sin, if you shit elsewhere...You know nothing yet of sterility or bacteria, the new enemy that might kill you.

When we're all grown up, we look back with our mental adult selves and remember—nothing! Not the instinctive knowledge of what really is good for us, not the complete trust we had and the confidence in ourselves and nature, and how reality felt before we were brainwashed by modern conceptuality...

Later we repeat the same uncooked stories to our own kids, of how bacteria, an invisible enemy, make us ill, how shit is something "bad" and how touching it is dangerous...

All parents repeat the postulates of their science, time and culture to their children with the reliability of a recorded tape, even the supposedly "politically incorrect" parent. It is just too lonely to be self-responsible!

Naturally, bacteria are not the enemy, nor are they hostile. Our guts are full of them, every kiss exchanges millions of them and they are all good and necessary, even the "bad" ones. A baby who tastes her poo (they don't eat it!) once or twice, receives a most valuable bio-feedback from that, which is important for brain-development and the development of digestive ability! She also receives a boost to her immunity towards bacteria and will later not react to bacteria like most people who are used to living in sterile isolation from life.

Your healthy baby will not get sick from tasting his poo, but he most likely will get sick from being vehemently stopped from doing so every time! A table-top, cleaned with disinfectant—that is truly a danger to the licking baby, but licking a rotten tree-log or their own droppings is not!

All you need to do to find this out is take your babies to a Filipino mountain tribe, where dog, chicken, pig and human shit is part of their daily world!

That is exactly what I did with my little daughters. Sure, they vomited and shat loose once in a four-month period, but they only got stronger from that initial clean-out! They didn't get divorced from all those bacteria, but learned to co-exist with them in harmony.

In fact, what looks like a lack of sanitation to the white man, is the cleanest environment this traveller has ever experienced! No chemicals anywhere! Everything is made from natural materials, except for the odd roofing-iron now making its way in.

Nothing here is wrong. People defecate in appropriate locations, not all over the place. There is no shit around the kitchens. Where natural communities are not yet pressured, everything functions perfectly and bacteria are good friends. People know how to keep their wounds clean and enjoy generally a free health service from nature and the village shaman. Their world is undivided. There is no bullshit, in fact many of those remote tribes have no idea what lying is, and thus no problems with shit as we do. No constipation, no haemorrhoids, no mean stench from "bad" shit.

Their poo is wonderful as a fertilizer for growing food, while our western shit must be seen as a health hazard.

Some tribal people are not yet divorced from their bodies and are heart- instead of head-centred.

They are undivided between inside and outside, between perceiving truth and expressing it.

You see babies playing with faeces and getting cleaned up by their siblings afterward, before they get uncomfortable. No stress around shit, sex, birth or death. It's all part of an indivisible whole...

We white people, or "westerners," have completely lost this kind of balance and wholeness and we take it away from those "pitifully poor people" as soon as we touch them. We tell them this is good and this is bad, stealing half of their world. We make them ashamed of their naked bodies, their bodily functions and their lack of what we define as wealth.

We do to them exactly what we do to our children!

I am immensely grateful for the existence of such bullshit-free peoples and for what we can learn from them about wholesome living and undivided reality! For my little ones I could never have found an environment cleaner or more beneficial in every respect, and what I learned there about babies and reality and community cannot satisfactorily be put into word or concept.

Babies like to shit freely where-ever they are and feel good about it! This is until we stuff it up for them...

It is of the highest importance to never let a baby spend any length of time in wet or full nappies, especially at night or when they sleep! At night, half an hour of such discomfort and loneliness and unanswered crying, is like an eternity to a baby, in which countless monsters can and will come into life!

Just imagine yourself lying in cooling shit and piss for a week and no way to change or end your helplessness...would you like that? Neither do babies.

The smell that goes along with the experience will be hated together with the shit, piss, cold wetness, loneliness and helplessness for the rest of this baby's later life.

However, as the recognition of this fact would put additional "pressure" on sleeping mothers, busy parents and psychologists choose to ignore it, if ever it dawns on them.

In my mostly outdoor environment, I solved these problems by using no nappies at all during the day, while being extra close and aware of signs at night. This kept their comfort maximal, so that whenever they did need a change of nappy, they gave clear and distinct signs, rather than being routinely whiney.

In summer, my girls were, when little, usually naked and mostly outside in the shade of fruit-trees, and in winter we had a fire going. A wooden floor wipes off easier than a nappy is to wash, dry and fold up...

Sure, when we went somewhere by car, we would use cotton nappies, but they usually waited until we had a stop, to give us a chance to keep their nappy dry, because they did not want to piss themselves, even when very small...

They were simply used to being clean always and never had time to feel "dirty."

They always let me know, when they were getting ready to piss or poo! Being able to tell, allows you to take nappy off, hold baby happily over potty, without rush, put nappy back on, still dry. Better than guess-work, you mothers of quintuplets!

They learned using potty like monkey learns peeling banana and it took very few floor-wipes before they had picked it up.

Laissez-faire does not work any better than control-tripping though. Tribal communities don't practise laissez-faire either, quite the opposite. They provide less control, but far more positive guidance than we do! Less policing and more positive example!

I never "potty-trained" my babies as such, nor do I "train" dogs! It is rather all about being in touch and respectful of their reality, to show an example and to co-operate from there.

My babies only ever cried when they had a good reason to do so, but very rarely. Babies never ever cry without a reason!

A baby will whimper when uncomfortable, but if you address such a subtle sign correctly, it will not cry all night! It feels understood! Just never let it stew in its excretions—and it will trust you and be happy. But first—you must trust your baby!

Keep that baby clean, but make it fun, not a quick duty! Let them really experience the element water and splash a bit! It is better to wipe the bathroom dry now, than your tears later, when she splashes out as teenager...

But use only water with some cider vinegar or borax to wash your baby, never soap or shampoos. Use borax for washing clothes, body, hair, floor, dishes and carpets, dear mothers of five!

My babies never had even a trace of rash, but still I oiled them up with wheat-germ and almond oil at least once a week.

Please never use chemicals from your supermarket on babies, like baby-oil and powders, UV-protection crèmes, skin lotions and the like! Keep them clean and away from disinfectants, carpet-cleaners, vacuuming and the like. Those are "shit!"

But when you find your baby poking into a sausage he has just brought forth under the dining-table, do not ever jump up in horror and dismay! Don't interfere! It is not your business! You may think him too stupid to know what he is doing. He is not! You are!

Your baby takes an interest for a reason! This is a very valuable and formative experience for your baby, even when she has a taste or a smear-test! She will not eat enough of the shit to get into trouble with bacteria and it does not take that much to wait and clean up calmly a little later.

Children's digestive systems are as yet undeveloped and they learn to adjust much faster when they are allowed this naturally intended bio-feedback, if they so choose.

From what I have observed, all very intelligent children like to play with their poo! Or may be playing with shit helps them reaching their potential intelligence by keeping it undivided...

Don't let your baby pick up from you that "shit is bad" and "stinks!" And let her play with her poo, let her smell it and take note what colour it is. It should be nearly smell-free and dark-yellow and look smooth and solid enough. Take note again after eating beetroot.

Encourage kids of all ages to look at their shit before burying or flushing it! Make them aware of sour, putrid and rancid smells and let them examine the texture. With their fingers and with instruments! To this purpose you need one of those toilets where the shit is visible before flushing, not one that has it sliding out of sight!

If you find whole undigested beans in their excrement, either ask them to chew more thoroughly or strike beans from their meals. If you find coins in baby's sausage, show them to baby and avoid giving food she cannot recognize...

Get your kids used to enemas! Use them when they are constipated, before fasts and when they get a fever... Always add a little olive oil or chamomile tea, which prevents the gut from drying out.

A kid can sometimes shit himself over fear or excitement when already going to school! Or accidentally along with a mighty fart! Make sure he feels okay then, or shame will stay connected with shit from there on.

But most importantly—keep your own distaste and stress around shit to yourself and don't infect your kid with it! Raise your child without the divisions and preferences that erase half of their reality and of what they like as good. A wholesome child enjoys shitting, has no negative feelings about it and lives it as one of the polarities of mind *and* body, up *and* down, inside *and* out. She can then grow up to be an "as-well-as" person instead of an "either-or" half-person, and will accept the wholeness of their reality as a birth-right.

She will then have no reason later to join a collective need to wear her pants fashionably down and the arse out, which is the "equal and opposite force" to the cultural demand of keeping the arse hidden…

Be aware that your child naturally does what is right, just like animals do! It is you who got it all wrong…

Never lie to your children for any reason! Bullshitting your kid makes her lose her sense of reality as much as does the alienation from her shit and her bottom self!

Kids need to be allowed or taught observation and acceptance of all parts of themselves and of all their functions. They need to be allowed to call things by their real name and to love truth! They need to be respected, not programmed! They need you to get real!

Get that and you will raise undivided and connected children with vital, inhabited bodies, fitting pants and sane minds!

Chapter 12: Is farting "okay?"

You're in an elevator packed with people. Unsuspected, one of those quiet but toxic farts escapes your control and is now freely shared with all. What should you do?

Own up, raise your hand and apologize? Unless you're a dishonest person who needs this kind of ownership as a spiritual practise—this doesn't really help anybody, though! Better to just look questions at your victims and slightly shake your head...don't look overly innocent though...

The best thing you can do here is to get over your embarrassment!

But what should you do if you become aware of a fart just before it can escape? Should you pass it or hold it in?

I would say—never hold it in! If you're a very caring person you can press the button and get out before it makes its way through your layers of clothes... And if you really, really care, you can simply adjust your diet—or use the stairs!

But does it actually hurt other people objectively to smell a fart or are they just hurt by their own negative projections?

This would largely depend on the quality of fart we are talking about... There are farts that can kill! If you are aware of your fart smelling foul or rancid, it is still always okay to fart, but it is not okay to visit public saunas or use trams and cosy little restaurants. Other people should have a choice between oxygen and methane...

The fart of a healthy child or adult is not something to worry over, to apologize for or to ever hold in, even when in company, since it is as natural as eating and burping and should not be seen as offensive. In an ideal world!

In fact, the farts of other people serve us as a warning-system and give our bodies information they can make good use of! If you smell somebody's foul fart, your body will fine-tune its own protein digestion, as it doesn't like this outcome of poor digestion in somebody else. Also, at least intuitively, an intense fart tells you more about business partners than weeks of research! Farting thus becomes a way we learn from each other and know each other and ourselves!

If you clearly fart more than other people, you need to change your diet or the way you eat. Some people fart like hell after eating beans or onions, fatty meats or sugary cakes, but it could be a TV-induced distraction from good chewing or unsuitable table-talk also. Whatever makes you fart a lot is a food or situation that makes you mal-digest. The gas making up the substance of a fart develops only when a meal is improperly digested and keeps fermenting in the bowel. Cut out foods you can't digest well, not for the sake of air quality, but to prevent more serious digestive problems from developing.

When we ask—Is it okay to fart—there is of course a biological answer and a societal answer, a factual and a "moral" one. Society leaves little doubt that farting is not okay. It is seen as uncultured, rude, disrespectful and mean, and farting at a job interview kills your chances as surely as farting before a one-night stand. How come?

The head breathes and so does your arse—what could be wrong with that?

What is wrong, objectively, is that "civilization" has overwhelmed perfectly natural body expressions and stifled our normal body processes with mental censorship!

The philosophical question of whether civilization can or should ever replace the demands of nature can be avoided here. What matters is—what works and what doesn't!

If we abide by societal rules, suppressing the impending fart, this fart does not really go away, no matter how great our control, and our respect, and our fine manners are!

The gas will go somewhere! When you squeeze your anus tight to hold a fart in, this fart will rise upwards in the body, as there is nowhere else to go! We then have flammable, toxic gas rising up, leading to belly-aches (which can be seriously painful in children!), to head-aches, to discomfort and distraction. How does that help in the board-room or in bed??

What does your iron control do beside screw up your gut, your face, posture and communications? And eventually, this fart, or what is left of it, is going to come back down again! Often it comes back doubled in strength, usually more demanding and always more unexpected...

Such a held-in fart can disable a man in bed or he will end a hasty performance with a mother of all farts as his after-play!

In any case, right or wrong—It simply does not work to hold a fart in! For biological as well as for societal reasons.

Nor does it work to fart nightmarish clouds under the noses of board members...

But there are better ways than holding in the offending gas!

First of all we need to realize that there are two basic types of fart—the loud fart and the silent one! People usually know what is coming and what type to expect. From this we can then develop our strategies.

The thing with silent farts is that they are the really stinky ones! There is a wise word, that freely translated from German goes:

Solomon and wise men think,

Noisy farts do never stink.

But beware the silent fart,

Say good-bye and quickly part!

There is valuable truth in this old saying. Silent farts are the work of anonymous, carefully disciplined and secretive people, who smile in elevators and never own their crimes.

A loud fart that gets everybody to look at you is honest, direct and gives fair warning of impending olfactory messages! It is the very secrecy which makes the silent fart so pestilent!

What seems quite unfair is that the honest, involuntarily loud fart is always immediately noticed and you can never walk away from it!

After a silent fart, the perpetrator often successfully sneaks out of his cloud or simply smiles and gets away with it, where the honest man always gets caught...

This is where fart-mastery comes in! A yogi or person who has mastered his body and the *art of slow release* to an adept degree can take an honest loud fart—and make it silent!

This is done much like you'd play the didgeridoo. You're sitting on this reservoir of air or gas and gradually let it go in mellow and constant dosages. Keep the frequencies just below the sound-barrier and your honest fart will flow out as silent as a "bad" one! This is no magic, just good body-awareness and a relaxed perineum. You can then fart according to your biological needs as well as in harmony with your cultural etiquette. You remain undivided, unsuppressed, undetected, in-offensive and—your own natural self...

If your farts are of the silent type—you should become more open and honest before you mix closely with other people! Sort out your digestion and other inner processes, before expressing your innermost self to others. Use stairs and private sweat-lodges. Don't mix onions and beer at parties. And stop smiling! Eventually, they're going to catch you, particularly if there are no more than two of you in one bed or elevator...

Learn to walk away before the event if you can't stay away altogether and simply don't eat at parties nor have fizzy drinks.

Talking about fart-mastery and honesty so abstractly, I probably should relate an experience I had at high-school when I was a year eight:

I had a desk-neighbour, who was widely respected as a master-burper and we had had strong competitions on who could fart and burp longest and with the best sound. We were both really good and he could even burp melodies. We practised by feasting up with "devil-salad and onion buns" at first break and later farted on command or listened for that "perfect sound ..."

One day, during French class, our sexy teacher was throwing around with quite personal French questions, when I suddenly felt this almighty build-up in my lower self! It wasn't localized, but gathered like a storm-cloud from everywhere, containing rolling thunder...

I couldn't have got out had I wanted to, so heavy was I with inevitability.

So I tried to let it go *long and quiet*. Soundless sound ...

I had had a really good day and was quite relaxed, but the volume and power I met with from the start still took me by surprise:

The fart started clean and full and very low like a wonderful bass, with that elusive perfect sound! It was as dry as a didgeridoo and as voluminous. I gave as little air as I could and yet the sound persisted on constant and full pitch, no rising or falling, no sign of weakness.

At first, I was still nervously aware of the sudden silence that had fallen over the classroom and of the teacher waiting furiously for me to finish, to then fall on me with some biting verbal assault on my fallibilities of character.

I considered of course the alternative manoeuvres—one was to apologize while the offending event was still under full steam, or I could have run out, every step a trumpet-blow, under the laughter of the class...It all seemed trivial, mousy and against nature...

I could have put the full cork in, but I knew this wouldn't work, would only break into unholy pieces, what was, I soon realised, a unique thing that should not be destroyed. So yes, I did responsibly consider the alternatives in those first moments, but without holding on to any and without a flinch in the tone of my rectal vibrations...

After a minute or so of undiminished perfect sound, the tension in the room had given way to wonder and astonished awe and I no longer felt like I was being rude or out of line!

I was a master! My neighbour looked at me with new-found respect and genuine admiration, even awe, and the teacher no longer looked like she had anything to say.

There was now a profound silence and still the thunder rolled on without the slightest gap, into the books of records and into the eternal memory of all who witnessed the event! Everybody was far too much in awe to check their watches, but a conservative guess would have clocked it at about three minutes and no boast intended.

When it ended, it did so with the precision of a concert instrument. It didn't trickle or fizzle out like lesser candidates. It suddenly ended in complete silence! People sat in trance for a quarter of a minute after that. They had witnessed the unfathomable...

And I was actually proud! Still today I am a little proud of this achievement of having created the longest and most perfect fart in living memory, before a stunned and awed audience!

I was never reprimanded by the teacher either, who obviously felt respect where respect was due for achieving excellence...

From that day, I certainly believed in my inner powers and found a new measure of self-acceptance. Soon after, I started with yoga and got into music...

What, may you enquire, is the moral of this "inappropriate" but honest little story?

The "moral" of this account is that it does not matter so much whether or not you fart!

What matters is how *well* you fart and how *honestly*!

I also learned that even a loud fart in public can be quite inoffensive, as long as you don't add your own apologetic embarrassment! You can make it into a work of mastery instead...

The "art of the soundless sound" is usually preferable, but if life happens—make the most of it!

In a tribal society where farting is okay, people know immediately when they start eating a difficult food or when somebody starts to mal-digest. They understand therefore a lot more than we do about each other, about food and about well-being.

To us, smells are mostly unpleasant, if we can at all smell anything. Throughout our "progress" through modern times, we have progressively lost our sense of smell together with our instincts and our intuition. What we call "progress" is really only a progress of matter and not at all of our human selves. We see and hear less than our ancestors; touching is mostly taboo, and smelling a lost art. Of all our senses only taste is sometimes cultivated where a person can avoid sugar.

The reason for this loss of our sense of smell is that we don't use that part of the brain any more that processes smells and intuition! Smell is processed by those same archaic faculties in the brain that modern man has switched off together with his non-rational animal-self. We are far too visual and mental now to be aware of subtle realities. Every dog will confirm this.

It also happens in reverse—by ousting our sense of smell into the land of shadows, we lose contact to those parts of our archaic brain even more, basically reducing brain-function.

If we knew just how much our emotional reality is determined by smells, we would not be as surprised at the cultural confusion that has resulted from the sterilization of all odours from our experience of life!

When walking into a hospital, the sterile smell that greets us is experienced as a smell of sickness and death by all children and all healthy adults. But walk into a horse stable and most people feel homely, trustful, warm, friendly and healthy! Sterilize that—and those feelings are all gone...

Only the fart of unbalanced humans, who eat junk food and sit all day, can objectively smell "bad." Or is there at all such a thing as an objectively bad smell?

Is it not rather all in the nose of the beholder?

While I admit that some farts challenge the assertion, it still needs to be said that "bad" smells, like also pain, are subjective experiences that are created by resistance against what *is*! If you have no resistance against the molecules in the air or against intense nerve messages, there are no evil smells, nor is there pain! I tested this under the dentist's drill without injections and found that as long as I don't fearfully project and judge what I might feel and utterly accept what *is*, I am completely without pain! Not without the sensation, but without the suffering! The same is true with smells, where the definition as "bad" is purely based on what we have learned to culturally reject and on our divisions from the "nether-lands" of reality. This is why some people hate and others love the smell of petrol or cow-shit, or of sweaty woman.

Smells simply connect with feelings and the more of them we dislike the more we reject what we feel about the world and ourselves.

There are no bad smells as such in nature except the smells of illness, of imbalance and of death. But even those smells are important and not to be casually avoided!

Dog can smell impending death and so should a good doctor! And if you have children, you can count yourself lucky if you are able to smell imbalances on them before they manifest as stronger symptoms! A "bad" breath and a "bad" fart often give us just the warning we need to protect our loved ones and therefore should be appreciated.

Is it then okay to fart during sex? Well, try not to, without running off to the "bathroom" to "powder your nose!"

If sex is shared with a trusted person who accepts you as you are, there is no problem. And if it is a one-night stand, a fart helps you to get real and learn to have sex only after you have established such trust and acceptance...

Barbie dolls, of course, don't fart, but real women do, especially when being rolled around and "noodled" and squeezed—always face the facts!

So farting is definitely not the crime we make it out to be and even less so when perpetrated by your kid at dinner. Get over it!

It was Martin Luther who once said to his dinner guests:

"Why don't you burp and fart? Did you not like my food?" I don't think the man was being unnecessarily crude there. He simply saw the connection between truthfulness, realness—and a good fart!

Chapter 13. Sex and shit

In nature's design, the arsehole is only two inches away from our genital organs. Nature thus makes it very clear how closely related the two are in their location, anatomy and function. To put it more bluntly—we piss through our genitals and we have sex with our arses!

And yet, many modern people indignantly and strictly separate the two functions as the "wrong way" and the "right way" or as entirely unrelated.

One may see the arse, as I would, to be no alternative to a vagina, but why disregard entirely the arse that comes *with* a vagina? One can be quite unconfused about their differences—but to keep the arse out of sex is no more sensible than keeping sensuality away from shitting! It ruins both!

When we tell the children our stories about "hell" and the evil "nether-lands" and finally succeed in separating them from their bottoms, this does not only affect their intelligence and their digestion. Those children are simultaneously brainwashed into thinking of sex as an equally stinky, slimy and disgusting affair as shit! It is a low-down base and likely sinful thing that does not bear open and honest discussion apart from distorting bullshit.

The psychology of shitting parallels that of sexuality to such a degree that the arse cannot be understood without sex and where good sex cannot be had without getting over arse-issues first!

People, who avoid thinking of shit around sex, are the ones who then get flatulent during love-making and will likely crown their quickie with a master-fart during orgasm!

They are the men who don't enjoy going down on a woman for fear of "evil" smells, and they are the women who slap the guy who farts in bed. None of the shit-haters really enjoy full-on sex or are very capable of it...

Sex and shit are suppressed by exactly the same cultural programs, which put the "nether-lands" to the South Pole. Thus we face an artificial cultural division between sex and shit that runs utterly against the grain of biological reality. This division demands, that shitting must not be sensual and that sex needs to be kept strictly away from the arse.

A person who challenges this strict division, like gays, women who like it up the back-alley and people who put a finger in the other hole during sex, is usually seen as "perverse".

Since you can't have good sex while you're still full of "shit," these strict divisions need to fall before you can enjoy the full potential of your sex-life! This is why any lover worth his salt will grab a woman's cheeks and caress her arse during sex, instead of whispering words of undying love into her already inflated head!

It is more often women who have serious arse-issues, or should I say the "ladies?"

A "lady" will often use perfume and deodorant to cover her womanly scent and any anal odours before having sex. This lady has definite arse-issues!

She attracts men who also prefer chemical perfumes over the intimate fragrance of the actual person they choose to make love to. These men will never accept her for who she really is, as they are mental lovers without an animal self or a personal interest. They are the same men who will faint in the birthing-room...

The type of modern woman who sends out those self-denying messages, gets only a very sterile version of what could be real sex and finds after a while, that "all men are equally useless" in bed. After all, she only knows the one type of man—the mental man she attracts.

The same woman is easily recognized. She never says the word "shit," nor does she ever go for a shit. She goes to the "bathroom" to "powder her nose!"

Avoid this woman, you red-blooded males, because all she wants is the white picket fence and duty-sex once a month!

Another sure sign, not that I advocate the practise, is how a woman reacts to a respectful pat on her behind, which has now become "sexual harassment," when a while ago it was received as a compliment! Why, do you ask, must a pious Christian lady see this necessarily as a gesture of disrespect? Why can she not turn the other cheek?

Most men judge sexual attraction by the shape of a woman's arse. If it is narrow, with the cheeks tightly clamped, they know a woman to be religiously un-sexual. If it is a happily swaying Jenny Lopez-wonder, they are sold!

And women are just as secretly fascinated by their bums when in front of a mirror or keep going on about their "fat" arses to make people look and respond with some contradictory compliment.

And yet we deny the arse as a sex-organ! It simply belongs to the other side of what we define as clean and proper sex and as an acceptable body-part.

We feel that shit has absolutely nothing to do with sex and we don't talk about shit before during or after sex to preserve this sterility. The ladies continue to "hate" their "fat" bums, farts, body-hair, socks and everything that goes beyond the clinically sterile sex-act they are prepared to perform.

I witnessed a very interesting experiment in trying to take shit-issues out of an evolving sexuality, when visiting a sex-commune in New Zealand. Their guru had after listening to the intimate accounts of hundreds of women realised what stopped them most from achieving orgasms with a man—lack of emotional honesty! Since many of the women at the community could in fact not orgasm or found it very difficult, he devised a few rituals that require absolute honesty with self and others. One of them was a weekly naked meeting, where intimate truths were being expressed, no bullshit allowed. People had to own their shit and no blaming on others or the government, God or the world. Another scheme of his was to teach the women to moan and groan on top of their voices during sex!

And the third one was to build four-in-one toilet units, where all privacy was relinquished for the sake of "social shitting!" I have rarely seen an idea work so well!

I'm generally a rather private person and prefer shitting alone somewhere in the bush. My own first experience in their public shitting was however a relaxed and rather pleasant affair. There were already three residents enjoying a most philosophical exchange while having a friendly dump, and my own arse made little difference to the setting. We all just had a good friendly shit and I was surprised at the level of wit that went along with it...

But there were other visitors! And I could not believe how agitated they all became when they were told and when they finally had to try out the shithouse! Although the seats were disinfected twice daily, and disinfectant always handy, people experienced all sorts of strange anxieties, that they tried very hard to hide and to rationalize away. They were tripping themselves into constipation and desperate bush-walks and into the "realization" of just how strange this "cult" was—faster than they could say "free sex ..."

From my observations it became clear that those who learned to become comfortable with non-private shitting also solved their sexual issues! They became emotionally honest! And all the screaming women learned to orgasm! Orgasm is indeed a function of honesty...

Although these "cultish" practises of sex-communes are suspect to many, they are but adaptations to what naturally happens in tribal communities!

I was quite used to giving up privacy in trusted environments, from living in such tribes. Used to express myself without censorship, used to nudity, and used to speaking and hearing the truth...

So I had no problem. But almost all New Zealanders I met at such sittings were struggling and many left the place in abject horror.

They would feel a lot worse in a mountain village, where pigs get at your sausage before it drops and where a lack of common language forces you into body-speak and facial expressions that cannot help but be utterly honest...

Don't think in our modern life there is no use for the ability to shit or piss without embarrassment! Think of that bus you stopped between towns, because you had too much to drink earlier...A hundred impatient eyes boring into your back and only two minutes to go before the horn tells you to finish! This is where the Catholic man starts sweating, while the pagan pisses happily and doesn't terribly care how long it takes...

All those things you learn in an animistic tribe apply somehow to our modern lives. I find that in order to get an idea on what is real and true and what is not, one has to live for a time with people who don't yet know what a lie is and who are as authentic as salt and earth. Then you notice that what modern man lacks most is personal honesty!

After a few months, you have quite grown out of your own cultural program and start seeing it for what it is. Eventually, you start seeing things without any cultural filter, for what they really are beyond your old or any cultural perspectives...

Then you realize how very little we really know or properly understand!

The main common denominator between sex and shit is clearly our issue with honesty and authenticity! Another one is that we know equally little of any value about either proper shitting or real sex!

This was not always so. Most great civilizations of the past have been built on sex- and mushroom-cults with the basic vision of a connection between Heaven and Earth, as symbolized by Nietzsche's eagle and snake, or the Aztecs' Quetzal-bird and snake.

The ancient Chinese Taoists as well as Indian Hinduism or the New Zealand Maori saw the world as a polarity between Heaven and Earth and spiritual advancement as a marriage between Heaven and Earth. Sexuality is the path to get in touch with the earth-bound snake and let it rise to the heaven or higher centres.

The Indians call this snake-energy "kundalini" and the Chinese call it Jing Chi.

Both cultures have known things about the potential of sexual energy for thousands of years, that our modern science and the general public have no hint of a clue about...

The Chinese look at the body in terms of energy-centres, or chakras as the Hindu yogis say, not just as flesh and bones. They have realized a few thousand years ago, that shitting and sex are ruled by one and the same first chakra, from which the energy of the central nervous system originates.

All spiritual development starts with this first chakra, the seat of kundalini, which connects us to the earth and to the truth. It is exactly half-way between anus and vagina or scrotum, at a definite point that the Chinese call Hui Yin. This point is the source of Jing Chi, from which all other chi is made by higher energy-centres.

All forms of human energy, like brain-activity, consciousness, and of course love and happiness—it all comes originally from the sex-chakra.

Where the sex-chakra is activated and fully functional, which has nothing to do with actually "having" sex, we receive replenishing vital energy in higher centres and in the whole body. We feel fresh, interested and sharp and life is going places!

If we instead go through life with a depressed, inactive first charka, we will feel tired, exhausted and easily stressed, since no Jing Chi is getting through. We will then likely have regular head-aches or suffer from migraine.

Most head-aches in women by far arise from conceptual suppression of a sexual or anal nature. Menstruation by itself does not do it, nor does it affect all women equally. Menstruation as such does not make the head ache. But hating the "mess," feeling handicapped, not wanting to be kept from mental performance by women's "problems"—that resistance against an otherwise easy and natural event is what causes the head-ache!

These head-aches cannot be cured by aspirin, only ignored.

In the West, the sacro-craniologist is the only scientist who is aware of this dependence of the head on an intact arse. He puts one hand on the occipital bones at the back of the patient's head and the other on the tailbone or below, achieving good results from connecting the two separate points of polarity. But the only permanent cure is to acknowledge our sexual and anal issues and to fully activate the first charka!

Don't worry, thou seekers of enlightenment, about those higher chakras yet, about the "hara" and the heart or the ability to see beyond this world with your third eye! None of this will work, before you are grounded! Without a clear and active first energy centre there is no higher development, only concepts of it. Like the "romantic" love of white picket fences and knights in white armour, or the "seeing of gods" strangely reminiscent of our suppressed devils...

The Chinese tantrics take a mostly physiological approach to anal deficiencies. They simply clear and strengthen the sex-chakra and activate it by flooding it with sexual energy without leaking energy out through ejaculation.

As soon as the sex-chakra is activated, a person is no longer trapped in the head and in conceptuality, but feels grounded, energetic and in full possession of his animal self.

This is the true beginning of a spiritual path that can lead to the activation of higher chakras and to higher awareness!

One of the most common mistakes of spiritual seekers is to start their journey conceptually with a fixation on the heart and love, or on seeing and higher perception! To do so only leads to confusion, to distorted perception and to mental spiritual fantasies!

Without being grounded to the earth by a functional root-chakra, there cannot be any valid higher perception, only conceptual head-stuff.

Many think that love has nothing to do with sex and that parental love should be valued above all sexual love. I don't disagree with that. You can develop love without sex, as people like Mother Theresa demonstrate. You can also be a thinker without being grounded and even be a wise man in a board-room. But there is no actual power to such love or insight, without grounding! It is like wanting to get light from Volt alone, without an earth-wire...

Mother Theresa, despite of her loving heart, had no sexual grounding and no Ghandi-like insights that she could have powerfully enough put to the world. She did not use her political power to change the world to any degree and instead perpetuated the status quo, where poor people continue to depend on hand-outs from "democratic" missionaries. She did not demand real change, as demand is not a heart-function.

The heart alone, as a focus of spiritual progress, can never replace a weak sexuality, but will remain aloof and unrelated to reality. You can only walk to heaven after you have learned to stand on firm ground! And you can only be grounded after letting go of your mental descriptions of reality and your centred-ness in the head. This is absolutely true, no matter what tradition you follow.

Most of us western folk follow a God of love and sin and shame, which clamps off our sexuality and realness for the sake of a conceptual, mental God that lives somewhere in the beyond. There is no real insight, no real power, no higher truth to be found in concepts handed down to us by religious traditions. Only faith adds some power, even where it is misplaced. If our faith precludes sex and the anal realm from participating in reality, religion becomes hostile to spiritual development...

The path to God is the path of practical self-development and there are certain steps that need to be taken. Grounding and the activation of Jing Chi is the first step and cannot be skipped.

When Jing Chi rises up to the heart eventually, the love you experience is no longer just a 'good feeling', but an elemental power to be reckoned with! When the energy rises to the brain, it then no longer manifests as furious concept-thinking, but becomes clear and unified consciousness, a connection between Heaven and Earth.

Every spiritual path starts at the beginning, not in the middle or "up there!" In order to work, it has to cultivate sexual energy and harness it for higher purposes, rather than suppress it as a "hellish" antithesis to the divine!

The techniques of activating the sex-chakra are simple and they work wonderfully! Basically, you draw your aroused sex-energy out of the genitals, back through the anal area and into the tailbone, without losing it via ejaculation. If the anus is psychologically blocked from feeling sexual energy, this cannot work—and you ejaculate. Only when the perineum and arse are allowed their own natural sensations without mental censorship, will Jing Chi arrive in sufficient measure at the tailbone and enter it through two little holes. These little holes need a solid blast of Jing Chi, not just a trickle, to open up for the first time. If you have a "blocked" arse, no energy can enter the spine and make its way upwards to the higher centres. This is why "religious" concepts hostile to sexuality stop us dead in our spiritual development. The Latin re-ligio means to re-connect, not to separate off! And re-connect you must, if you are to get somewhere.

Only when sexual energy grounds you to the earth, can you have a connected polarity and the resulting electricity to see the light...

Shitting and sex are those functions that if cultivated properly, bring us down to earth, to reality and to the realization of truth. Spiritually, the first chakra is all about openness and honesty! This is what we are working with on a psychological level, while doing the energy-work. Without dedication to truth the head cannot let go of itself…

If only "truth" were not so utterly excluded by our cultural dogmas…

They lock you up if you are emotionally honest these days! It is just not done!

As a result, the sperm count of men in New Zealand and the US has fallen by sixty per cent in the last twenty years! Prostate-, cervical-, and breast cancers are epidemic and women's fertility and libido have dropped considerably. This is our reality check!

Nobody looks at how obviously these changes and illnesses relate to our collective beliefs about anal and sexual reality. We blame environment and chemicals, not realizing that the damage we do to ourselves far exceeds even the damage done to the environment!

No chemical medicine can help here. All we can do to escape physical and spiritual extinction is to restore natural attitudes around our arses and to get over our insane sexual attitudes. We need to bring Heaven and Earth together, not continue to create a gulf of Heaven and hell for ourselves and our children!

Allow yourself the sensuality to let shitting be fun! It is the next best thing to having sex before breakfast.

Chapter 14. Dieting and real shit

Anybody who has tried it for some time knows that dieting does not work.

None of those many advertised diets work! Dieting is a mental imposition on our senses, a mental control of non-mental functions that is only ever tried by people already deeply separated from their bodies.

Dieting is a marketing plot, just like the "new age" is now mostly a marketing plot, selling concepts.

Correct diet is something that has to be sensed and figured out by the individual, according to her unique needs and purposes! A Jenny Craig or Atkinson diet can never fit your personal requirements, nor does it affect different people in one and the same way. It follows a general theory that will not fully suit any one person who tries it.

To follow a prescribed diet in the hope of losing weight is to follow an illusion.

It is quite impossible to lose weight in the longer term through dieting and a planned reduction of calories! The less you eat, the more your metabolism slows down, going into survival mode, and you need less and less calories to maintain the same body-weight.

As soon as your mental control over what you desire then slips, as control always does, you regain your previous weight as fast as you can say—bugger Jenny!

This is at the root of things so because body-size and weight are an expression of who we are mentally and emotionally and not a mere function of calorie intake. Overweight people are big for psychological reasons, mostly because they believe in continuous maximal growth, rather than the reality of death...

Some people may want to grow the attention of others for their bodies, others grow a physical self-importance to hide inner insecurity, but generally they share a common focus on the material world, at the expense of their inner selves or to be exact—of their astral selves...

If you are an intense dreamer, who dreams in bright colours, possibly lucidly, your astral body, which is the body you walk around with in dreams, is strong and holds much of your energy. You stay skinny physically.

But if you never recall your dreams upon wakening, never give them any attention, or if they are just unimportant foggy things that befall you on occasion—then your astral body loses much relative importance and some energy to the physical body, which then starts growing out of proportion to your astral self and to its own normality!

So, forget dieting if you want to lose weight! Dieting is to focus on your material, bodily, measurable self ever more, pitching it up to cult-like importance!

What you need, if you want to really become a smaller person, is to shift your mind away from your worldly, superficial, external money- and body-perspectives and towards who you really, honestly are emotionally and spiritually!

To look at mirrors, scales and calorie tables further reinforces your mechanistic world view and will set you up for further weight-gain! Look instead into your heart and ask—who am I emotionally, when I'm not the "fat lady?" Who am I as a spirit and a dreamer, a lover, as a non-material person? Who am I in the hour of my death?

This shift of focus will change and adjust your metabolism and your body-weight simply because your physical self begins to weigh less on the scale of who you are as a whole person! Energy always follows attention and so does body-weight.

It is very simple. The more astral you are relative to the physical and the ethereal, the skinnier you will be. What scientists fashionably call "genetic predisposition" is simply a structure for and a way of looking at—consciousness, personality and ways of thinking...Genes are not something apart from consciousness, nor do they determine reality independently of our long-term choices.

So, if you don't want to make your own personal and responsible inner choices, but keep joining the collective fascination with the consumption of the material, physical world—then of course your material side, the body, keeps growing beyond the normal! Is that surprising?

There is of course some trickery—you can influence the chakras, which medicine calls the "endocrine glands," by stimulating ovaries, gonads, adrenals or the thyroid gland. This simulated chakra-activity makes people more "astral," thus losing physical weight.

But forget trickery we don't even understand! Forget trying to find external, chemical or mechanical solutions to obesity! It is the root-cause of obesity to focus on those external things in the first place, and the only definitive cure is in exploring instead who you are inside, beyond the body and its weight!

To throw away your scales is the best start. You lose weight straight away by just doing that...

But, you ask, is there no perfect diet as such? Of course, there is! You can find the right food for yourself by re-awakening your natural instincts!

Until then, you need to watch your shit! If a "diet" makes you poo loose or constipated, it cannot be good for you. If it is green and slimy, makes you fart or if it sinks quickly—this diet isn't for you.

At this stage, you cannot trust your instincts yet, undeveloped as they are, so you cannot just go by taste. But by eating only natural, unprocessed foods you cannot go far wrong.

I recommend leaving the head out of eating and use it only for shopping!

Don't buy whitened wheat products and repetitious steak. Buy millet, quinoa, wild rice, sweet-corn and all the grains you can come by. Such greater variety will challenge and strengthen your digestive abilities, balance your enzyme-levels and your peristaltic movements!

Eat a large variety of meats, inner organs and many different seasonal fruits and vegetables. Avoid food from the supermarket, as it is mostly crap.

Eat to your satisfaction and always with gratitude, then watch your shit and stick with what gives you the best sausage...

This is all there is to diet for weight-loss, apart from the fact, that dieting is nearly always done for the wrong reason.

To most people's mind dieting is the only answer to their desire to lose weight!

As I said upstairs, you cannot lose weight for long through dieting. But the more massive illusion here is that weight is at all the problem!

Body-weight has as such absolutely no effect on health or on sexual attraction.

Only being fat does!

The complete avoidance of the fat-issue by most females has us talking about "weight" and thereby we entirely miss the point...

What could be wrong with a female hammer-thrower at a hundred kg of hard muscle? Why would she want to lose weight? To attract some skinny guy in fear of so much real woman?

On the other hand, there are thousands of skinny white girls, that have flabby abdomens and soft, unused flesh, who are clearly too fat at fifty kg!

The real issue here has never been weight, but firmness! Proportion and firmness of flesh is what decides how healthy and attractive a person physically is. Weight is completely irrelevant and a misleading concept! There are absolutely stunning big people!

Before electricity came to Samoa, I stayed for a while at the "fale" of the High Chief of Savaii, learning language and culture. The girl-pressure was pretty intense, but one day the chief's oldest son decided to introduce me to a "real Samoan woman," not one of those "skinny girls you go off with," as he put it.

This *real woman* weighed in at about 150 kg, had a beautiful face, Angelinic lips, and a warm, womanly personality. I did end up spending the night with her and it was one of the best sexual encounters of my life...She had no flab at all, no fat anywhere, only very firm flesh, hard as truck tyres! Her breasts must have been fat-tissue, but they were huge and standing hard and she had four-inch nipples from still breastfeeding her seven-year old daughter. I had never seen such firmness on a skinnier woman, nor such breasts without a major sag...she was a true Goddess! A "real woman" indeed...Even when she was on top, I thoroughly enjoyed this much woman, even when I worried somewhat over the bed almost collapsing under my skinny arse...

Since then I have felt sorry for the soft, skinny girls in the west, who eat white bread and sugar, and then diet and never move much... Their flesh is sickly un-firm and they don't smell very good!

They are usually more fat than muscle, at any given weight...

What they need is certainly not more weight-loss, but a life-style that makes their flesh useful, instead of a mere decoration!

Compared with a tribal woman, the white girl is fat, really, and very few white people have a pleasant smell... This is in no way a race-preference, but rather a dog's point of view...

Over-eating as such is never the problem either. As long as you work it all off, you're just fine eating as much as you like! The problem is only with a mentality that eats for the wrong reasons and with a hunger for emotional things that cannot be eaten...

If you want your body back, if you want to reconnect with your natural balance—you need to see your body as part and extension of your inner self, rather than as a possession or a replacement for inner realities. You need to abdicate your cultural obedience to being a materialist and to seeing yourself as "the body."

Once the weight of material things on your scales of life diminishes in favour of more inner consciousness, your body-weight will reduce together with your appetite for all the wrong things you do not need.

Don't even check your weight! Throw those scales away and check your body by pinching your arm to see if it is flabby or capable of doing a day's hard work!

And check out those beliefs and unlived emotions that make you look at your body with distaste or as a decoration to flatter your ego...

If you want to look good—*be* good! There is no chemical trickery...

There are of course diseases that require a specific diet, but this diet alone cannot cure any disease. To the cancer patient I would like to say this much:

For early self-diagnosis watch out for green, but more importantly for red, black, light or white stool! Red is from fresh blood at the end of your colon, black from blood higher up, a light colour shows problems with the gall-bladder and a white product could likely announce pancreatic cancer. Don't for a moment think you can correct the colour with food alone! The correction needs to be emotional and psychological, bringing about a changing world-view.

You then also need to find your own balanced, natural diet with your own senses. Don't follow somebody else's theory! To you it is about taking full responsibility for yourself!

The same rules of common sense apply to you as they do to everybody else. Don't buy chemical-loaded foods from the supermarket, of course. Avoid cheap eggs, caged chicken, caged pork, denaturalized milk, white bread, sugar, certainly. It is vital to eat good lively food from your garden, sure.

But to think this more sensible diet will cure your cancer is a wishful fantasy! It is just one factor that needs correction, but no cure. Even "magical trickery" with ginger, parsley, garlic and ant-oxidant berries and purple sweet potato will not cure cancer.

This total focus on diet as the main alternative to chemical warfare is just another subscription to blind materialism, that looks for solutions in material things, external forces, chemicals and other people's white coats! Even new-age healers promote mostly external cures and subscribe to the fashionable food-mania, without realizing how they reinforce the patient's belief that cure comes from the outside and from somebody else.

To cure cancer, you need to embrace what has been suppressed, suffocated or left unexpressed. See what you have never looked at!

Nothing starts to suddenly grow into a tumour without having been suppressed or depressed first. No yang exists without a previous, exceeding yin.

Looking at food with suspicion and imposing a mentally devised diet will never help you! To beat cancer, you need to mature spiritually and learn the life-lessons you have culturally avoided.

But for those who don't mind a bit of "magic" that is far beyond anything medicine can offer—here is a method for getting at the inner causes for cancer without the need to be a genius or to have supreme awareness: Smell, and look at, your shit!

Looking at shit is like looking at blood. Why is it that many people, after having a blood-test, even if it turns out inconclusive, suddenly feel better? Why did doctors ever think in the past that letting blood is a cure-all? The reason for this is that looking at your own blood triggers a myriad of magical possibilities in your brain...

War veterans will confirm that one of the greatest horrors on the battle-field is the smell of blood! It affects us in our deepest core, which is why all shamans use blood to affect changes in the mind/body...

Nothing stimulates wound-healing like the sight of blood.

Smelling our shit has similar effects! You may not be able to smell your early lung-cancer in your shit. But dog can! Which means the information is there, in the smell!

It has been scientifically proven that dogs reliably detect early cancer from smelling the shit of people!

But even we humans detect this same information, although it doesn't become conscious, since we don't use the part of the brain that dogs use. The difference is not the nose but the brain! But although subconscious, the human brain still registers the message!

To detect cancer via smell also means that every detail of how it is caused is part of this olfactory message! This means that our subconscious minds register all this information as a bio-feedback which directly leads to an increased awareness in the body of what is wrong and of how to adjust it.

The sense of smell does primarily address the emotional side of the cure. There is one even more effective step you can take in this direction—using your sense of taste, which relates directly to understanding! You can taste your shit!

If you think dogs don't know what they are doing when they eat their shit, you couldn't be more wrong! Eating even a tiny amount of your suspect shit will actually correct your digestion and immunise you against succumbing to the unusual or unsuitable food and bacteria you may ingest in the future! I hear you screaming...Eating shit? Well, nothing could be more natural or more effective! Or dog and most other animals wouldn't do it!!

There are many more applications of shit as a healing substance. A witch-doctor might apply shit onto chakras or other body-parts, or even smear it onto the face—with amazing results...but taste is the most effective.

You don't have to swallow! Holding it in your mouth and tasting it will close the cycle and give the body all necessary information. Your self-healing forces then have the necessary directions and are clear about their task. This will give you your best chance of actually dealing with the inner causes that created your cancer!

Chapter 15: Economical shit

Before we can talk about putting the shit back into economics, we first need to take some bullshit out of economics!

Today, everybody talks so much about "economics" and the "economy" – the word now does challenge the shit-word in popularity! Is that because we know as much about economics as we know about shit? Absolutely! Almost nothing...

So let us do what nobody does and re-examine what we actually mean by what we all say! What is really an "economy?"

We hear from our "economists" that what makes up an economy is—land, capital, labour, technology and "resources." The goal is to grow maximum volume...

These definitions are imprecise, incomplete and blatantly ignore reality as it in fact presents!

Our understanding of the value of land has with our loss of appreciation diminished to now be limited to a monetary value as "real-estate" or as a place to dig for minerals.

"Capital" is not in itself real! Money is only worth something by *representing* existing food, buildings, technology. If all those things are gone, money becomes worthless!

Capital and paper-values do not contribute to the real economy; it just makes our fantasies run faster!

The value of "labour" entirely depends on the direction this labour takes!

If a nation works hard and successfully in the manufacture of weapons or environmental poisons, then despite the achieved so-called "growth," there is still zero value in that labour for the real world-economy! Common sense should tell us that...

What value has the "labour" of a chainsaw-man in the Amazon, of a George W. Bush in Iraq or of the builders of Israel's wall? According to the "economists"—lots of value!

In reality, this misdirected labour needs to be undone at even greater cost! Sure, probably by somebody else, but we can't think like that any longer.

The value of any technology equally depends entirely on its direction! How can a technology of nuclear, biological and chemical weaponry "contribute" to the world's economy??

How does the replacement of communication skills with mobile phones for teenagers "contribute" to the world economy? According to economists, those things "grow" our economy...

In reality, they reverse the evolution of speech...

Instead of creating world wealth, such misconceptions create immeasurable costs—Invisible debts to the future, that evade every balance sheet...

Check out what economists mean by "resources!" Minerals, oil, gas, coal—all those things that feature on a company's balance sheet... We only define as "resources," what we today, in our blind, ungrateful, greedy corporate world-view recognize as useful to our profits in the short term.

In real life, an economy is what the living planet supplies us with for free:

Land, oceans, rivers, forests, sunlight, rainfall, wind, topsoil, clean air, intelligence, living things...

These are the real factors that make up an economy! All we can add is supportive "labour" and a healthy attitude that can lead us to a natural and self-sustaining technology. Such efforts do exist in some places, which leaves the definition of our world economy hinged on what nature freely supplies, minus what we have destroyed and keep destroying every day with our capital, our labour and our technology! Plus, what a few decent people grow, like rice, or young minds and healthy ideas...

To see land value in terms of short term gain as "real-estate" or for its industrial use only, loses ninety per cent of the true value, along with any appreciation of beauty and respect for creation.

Our economists' views, and those of the land-sellers, have devaluated land and as a consequence of their philosophy we have devastated the landscape wherever we went!

We hollow out the earth and stuff her bowels full of millions of tons of plastic and four-year old computers; we take most of her trees, kill her life-forms and pollute the rest with poison...

While choking the rivers with our shit, with dissolved anti-depressants, and with oestrogen!

What we don't realize is that all the damage we have caused by following this economical fantasy of ours, translates into real costs! Huge costs!

The cost to eventually repair the forests, the rivers and to clean up the oceans full of molecular plastic—all that cost belongs to the other side of that ledger, where we have presumed our profits to exist for decades!

Our arrogant definition of "economics," that utterly ignores the rising costs of many, many trillions of dollars' worth in damages, is not only obsolete, but endangers our survival more than any other threat today!

Once we start cleaning up our rivers and oceans and the very air we are supposed to breathe, we will begin to understand just how much cost we are facing!

When we re-grow the Amazon and our other forests, which will have to be done, we will see what our profits and our growth really were—insane illusions!

If we don't grow back the trees, we will need to filter carbon out of the air ourselves and put oxygen back, at far higher cost! If we at all can...

What is the use of cars, TV, computers and hamburgers, when we are left with un-breathable air, with water we can't drink—and hungry people whose corn gets eaten by cars?

The real economy has to include all those future costs of repair! Because repair it we must!

This does not mean that we can do it, though ... How do we bring back all the species lost by radical logging? Since all human technology is but simple imitation of what we observe from nature, every species has information we can't afford to lose! Without seeing birds, we can never invent the air-plane...For the profit of selling the wood from the felled forest we lose a hundred species, worth a million times more in the long term! For the transport of oil, we pay with spills that destroy the oceans and the shorelines. These losses are absolute and forever shrink our potential economy...

The idea that the world economy grows if we all consume more and spend more money, shows just how ludicrous our house-keeping really is! What we expand by spending is the bubble that will surely burst, but not the real economy!

Economics as we have it is particularly dangerous because it is about to establish itself as the world's leading religion, beating science, shopping, and all our other strange gods into their places...

If we take a more intelligent look at what an economy really is, we soon detect vast amounts of undiscovered resources of great value that our economists are not even peripherally aware of!

We cannot guess at the value and the possibilities of a forest! To see only its timber value ignores it as a habitat for thousands of species, as a water reservoir, as a carbon fixer, as an oxygen producer, as a restorative human habitat, as a classroom! Should we not first see how much value is in fact in such resources, before we burn them all...?

The same is true for water—it has a true value far above what we grant it in our "economical" contemplations. We haven't begun to tap into the richness of the oceans and already we are losing them...

We still bury our rubbish, blind to the fact that it is another major untapped resource.

Some smart people have recognized sunlight as a main economical factor and will keep discovering better and new applications of sunlight. Yet most of us still cannot grasp that energy does not need to be manufactured, but is intrinsically free and unlimited...

Even our own children's potential intelligence is a greatly undervalued resource that our ideas of education and economics blatantly ignore! What would happen if we stopped shovelling our antiquated views down their obedient throats in head-centred schools and instead allowed them to develop their own observation skills and perspectives, their own world views? One only has to experience the maturity of a nine-year-old tribal child compared to our sixteen-year olds, to know what I mean... Or be whipped on the chess board by Filipino jungle kids who have never been to a school...

Bringing out the human potential through proper development of mind, body and soul is an idea that has rarely ever been tried and we would not today "invest" in such "alternative" things of "questionable" profit... One more pillar of the *real* economy overlooked!

Another major undiscovered and mismanaged resource is the roughly two million tonnes of human shit we produce daily! At the moment all this shit is not just wasted, but flushed into rivers and into our ground water, where it creates a real threat and huge clean-up costs for our children! Such costs could all be shifted to the profit side of the economy by recognizing shit's true value...

A view that ignores human waste as something smelly and unworthy we should not talk about, inevitably leads to distortions of reason and is unaffordable to the *real* economy!

Objectively, shit is a highly valuable commodity! It has been used throughout time by non-industrialized cultures as a building material, as paint, mosquito-repellent, sun-protection, a cosmetic and for many other purposes.

Guano, the droppings of bats, has long been highly valued as a growing medium of unparalleled quality.

Composted, human poo too is a great fertilizer for growing food, which is why the Chinese have done it for thousands of years.

In the west, of course, where people live off hamburgers, fries and sugar-drinks, our shit cannot be expected to be very rich in nutrients. Nor is such a "gross domestic product" very hygienic to work with...

But I have grown all my fruit-trees in holes I used for a month as a toilet and left to rot for a year, with a bit of lime sprinkled on top. Works like a charm and no need to buy dubious fertilizers!

When my girls were little and their deposits as pure as roses, I grew wonderful capsicums and blueberries from their composted droppings, and as they watched they saw the *value* of their poo with pride and their place in nature with understanding.

Just visualize the daily pile of shit from six billion people! Should that continue to go into the world's rivers, you think, or should we grow food from it for a starving world???

Even the faeces from not so healthy people could be sterilized, dehydrated and shipped to where people try to grow food on sandy or rocky soils! Nothing is easier than to get rid of all smell! The houses in Africa that are thickly coated with shit don't hardly smell at all!

Neither do the cooking fires in Tibet, where dry dung is used instead of wood.

Shit is so versatile! It is right up there with bamboo and coconuts once you think about it...In New Zealand we actually have a newspaper made entirely of bull-shit! A farmer raising bulls for breeding found that he can make paper from his enormous piles of bull-dung! So he did just that and now runs a paper literally full of bull-shit! How wonderfully creative is that?

Alternatively, we could use human waste as an energy source! Anybody who has ever lit up a fart and singed his flaming ball-sack has some idea how much good energy we are not tapping here!

No, we can't walk around with condom-like contraptions, trying to catch our or other people's farts, but we may one day in the future have toilet bowls with airtight lids, that suck shit, gas and urine into separating containers, to be processed into our autonomous, multi-sourced energy systems...

Or further in the future – "smart clothes" using gases, body-heat and sunlight to convert into air-conditioning, colour-changes and partial invisibility...Wait and see!

Shit is simply too valuable to ignore in a world of limited resources. Why not drive our cars on it, instead of on corn? It can already be done.

But actually, in an ever hungrier world, shit is even too valuable to run our cars with! The most economical use for shit in the future is in the growing of food, especially since supply always stays proportional with rising demand...

The economy is much like a paddock with a cow. If you always take the shit away from the paddock, the milk produced is going to get less and less...

As long as the waste gets back into the ground, the grass will always grow.

In other words—the planet needs your shit!

Chapter 16: Shit like a master

When you become conscious of your actual shit, you also become conscious of "shit" where it is emotional and mental! You can then empty it out.

While most spiritual traditions tend to *fill you up* with their definitions and dogmas and feed you ever more things you need to acquire and become, or atone for, before you have a right to meet God - the Taoist path of "empty yourself of shit" frees you from programmed pre-conceptions, illusions, false gods and from fundamental division! Best of all—it overcomes our original division at its root—the division between head and arse, God and Earth.

When you free up and awaken your kundalini-energy, which is only really possible with an unencumbered arse, you truly are on your way to enlightenment! Reading the bible, the Qu'ran, or even the Upanishads cannot do that, and neither can Raja yoga, altruism or chanting Hare Krishna do a thing for you, unless it comes from the arse and from the gut...

To fill new and even better programs into your head cannot help, as they will always remain conceptual, head-based and therefore without power. All concepts lead to division—but enlightenment happens only when you are no longer divided!

Oneness is not "achieved," nor does knowledge ever approach it. It is the natural state! When we stop dividing things, we see that.

A person serious about walking the spiritual path needs to seek out not what makes her feel "good," and whatever is huggable, but where her strongest divisions—and restore their eternal oneness! It is that simple.

Once we get over our habit to divide the world, all things change. All "others" become simply human beings, as we belong to no group.

There are then no wars, as there are no "others" to fight. No war of the sexes, as we do not identify with our gender. No sexual diseases, because there is no sin-fearing, shameful, or casual energy in our earth-chakra that could produce them, or be affected by them. There are no digestive disorders, since eating and shitting work in harmonious context to each other.

Is this not a better platform from which to look out for God, or simply for happiness and health? Or do we truly think that listening to priests, or to ever more novel concepts, will help us practise and perceive oneness?

To master the human condition is to be undivided. Which means also—undivided from nature! You can never find God or higher awareness without walking through the doors of nature!

God's true "word" is written for everybody at every time—not in books that exclude all those who lived before the book was printed and those who can't read—but into creation itself and into our own natures! Shit is such a door of nature that can and must lead to the real thing ...

If you are alienated from your sexuality or despise your own shit, you are living against the external and your internal nature, and against the manifested word of the creator! From this divisive position you cannot possibly grow spiritually or see any light...You're then living in a dark tunnel.

The beginning of the *path* is to activate the first chakra. To skip this first step and getting all "advanced" with higher energy-centres, will always, after much painful disillusionment, get you back to step one.

A true master thus always owns a developed sexuality, whether he "has" sex or not, and he is of course a master at producing the perfect sausage!

The master will sometimes use his dreaming to correct himself, should he have eaten something "funny" while in the city.

If you eat the wrong food, you will promptly dream about eating! Dreaming about food always means that something is not quite right, for any dream-message needs a reason to exist. Just watch the symbolism your subconscious mind employs and you will get the precise message!

Dreaming about a feast means thus that you ate too much while talking, whereas a dream about poison in bread likely points you to a chemical-sensitivity.

I once erroneously killed "Verdura Frankenstein" in a dream, after eating lots of raw Mexican vegetables and then getting the runs. It made me realize that my "rational" conclusions to suspect the greens as the "monster" were wrong—and I kept eating greens successfully, eventually finding the true cause.

Dreams are one of our greatest sources for "inventions," insights, and true answers whether our questions relate to health, to body-size, or to spiritual growth. They are, like shit, an *under-ground fast track* to self-awareness that is usually put aside together with our fear of darkness and our insistence on alarm-clocks.

Even dreams are only clear, when we are not too full of shit however.

The master uses his dreams, as he uses everything nature offers, to complete his awareness. He does not divide dream-time from the rest of "reality!"

He gets his information everywhere, all the time, from all parts of nature.

It is not beyond him to taste his shit therefore, or lick his wounds, and to generally learn from dog, who knows many things. He is not divided from dog.

Like dog, he knows the suitable foods, and eventually all foods to him are "good" as long as they are natural. He could probably digest even a McDonald-burger without raising a stink, but finds better things to eat. He likes to feel fresh after a meal.

You can experience this bowel-freshness of the blessed man for yourself, tomorrow, if you so choose! Cleanse your gut with saltwater and follow up with butter-rice to prevent drying of the gut-walls. This flushing will bring out things like old lentils and other undigested foods you ate the year before and that clog up your nutrient-assimilating membranes. It can stink badly, but this is good! Better outside than in ...

The next morning you will shit the most beautiful, perfectly shaped and divinely textured, yellow banana of your life and absorb much better from there on! You will feel fresh...

You can do quite a few physical things to maintain great shitting: In the morning, after a glass of water and stretching, do the "cobra" or rock the body on your stomach.

Proceed to a shoulder- or head-stand, reversing your inner pressures, while breathing deeply.

Then stand upright, draw in your belly and let it pop back out a few times (banda).

Finally, do eighteen anus contractions.

You will shit like a champion after this, every morning, and improve your physical health considerably!

Just shit once a day and eat an apple afterwards, or a papaya, or black currents if you also have asthma, and you won't easily constipate from there on. No need to push or pull or to read your news in solitary confinement...

The "Running Man" can do the same routine, only eat a banana instead—and he must oil his arse well before the saltwater cleanse!

There are many practical, common-sense measures we can take on our path to self-improvement, but in order to become a master, we need to make shit our valued ally and learn to read from it all it has experienced on its journey through our inner selves!

To be blessed with perfect digestion is only a side-effect of the greater possibility of regaining our lost integrity and finding oneness by becoming conscious of *the other side* of what we usually focus on...

The ultimate goal is to bring light into the darkest corners of our psyche, that we never had the *guts* to explore! This is where you find the true blessing that makes the master!

He can look at the dark side...he always sees both sides of a truth and he is utterly committed to inclusive truth!

If you desire to shit like such a blessed soul, you will need to escape the world of mutually exclusive opposites by overcoming your division between head and arse.

This requires you to drop all the divisive programs you have been fed, your cultural world-views and all your exclusive club memberships.

Only then can you see truth beyond projection, beyond cultural and religious mirror-images, your divided, isolated ego, and other narrowing horizons.

Then you can squat easily behind a bush, drop the perfect banana, not needing a single leaf—and come out smiling rather than smelling! Then your mind is open, simple and grounded enough for higher perception!

And only then can you really start becoming aware of your higher self, your heart, your deeper understanding, and live the realities of all your energy-centres...

There can be no clarity of mind or heart before all the accumulated bullshit is out of our heads and put back down to the earth together with our real shit! Not enough clarity to discern the path...

As long as we disregard big parts of reality and split the rest into conflicting halves, we don't accept ourselves or others. We annoy each other and are confused as to the reasons why. But our subconscious mind, which contains all of reality, including our suppressed sex and shit, is quite unconfused about those submerged contents, and expresses them every time we lose some of the mental control needed to hold them under...

When we get scared or annoyed, rationality retreats and we call each other "arsehole" or "shit-head," because that is the electrically strongest and wisest message that arises from our "dark-lands." We aim to say the most hurtful truth, when we say these things—and there it is! What an offence, to call somebody an "arsehole ..."

The truth hurts—but only as long as we fight it and only *because* we fight it!

Accept that you are also your arsehole—and the offence disappears...

Acknowledge the "shit" that has risen to your head, when a mate helpfully calls you a "shit-head"—and the offence becomes an act of true friendship and an opportunity for growth!

Swear-words and jokes always cheekily express those parts of reality that our rational, cultural mind rejects, because they are products of our suppressed subconscious content, that can never be completely muted.

Why say the Germans—Scheisse, and the French—merde—at every occasion? Why do the Spanish most commonly offer shit-heads a —come merda—which is an invitation to eat shit? Because this is the best clue they can receive from their collective subconscious minds and the best advice to give to shit-heads! Why else?

Always look at what you leave behind! Don't flee that darkness! Light cannot exist without darkness...

Only in the dark has the light of a candle any power and only darkness can appreciate its gentle beauty!

Learn to look both ways, not only when you cross the street, but in all walks of life! You will then read loaded words like "evil" from right to left as "live," your famous "devil" as what you have "lived" in the past, and you may even find "good" and "God" in the eyes of your loving "dog ..."

You can happily walk up a hill and then down into a valley, without feeling down over this part of your walk...

This is how life works—its electrical power exists between positives and negatives and only if you bring these opposites together as one, can you see the light!

The mark of a "master" is simply that he acknowledges all his cultural automatism and gets over them. A "come merda" cannot offend him. He sees it as good advice and may say "thanks, done that last week..."

There is no more to it than to drop all your and other people's bullshit and to experience the superb clarity of the resulting wonderful emptiness...

You may fear that when you're really empty of all you've ever been told, and if you achieve an undivided mind—you would no longer be yourself!

The person you have known all of your life...

Your friends might not recognize you—and you would feel lonely...?

But are you not lonely already, in all of your divisions? And do you really know yourself now? Can you even guess who you really are underneath all that bullshit?

In truth, all you can ever "empty out," are those second-hand descriptions of the world, and your parents' prescriptions for life—all those things that are not you, at the core!

When you let go of all this arbitrary software, you are left with the actual hardware, which is who you really *are* in essence!

The emerging master is not a new and alien and oh so unattached person. He arises in the recognition of having always been there all along, underneath the mental fog, the divisive views and the loud voices screaming for ever more...

The master is who we are beyond all division. When we look at our droppings on the forest floor—and see food for plants and trees! When we see no "evil," but only a cycle of good. There has never been any evil. Only ignorance and division!

The common denominator of all worthwhile spiritual paths is to overcome this polar division of reality. Christ points at our division from each other and at love as the means to transcend selfish boundary. Lao-tzu teaches to see all things in connected and inter-changing pairs of yin and opposite yang. And the Zen-masters transcended the wall between reason and non-linear reality by asking you to listen to the sound of one hand clapping...

For modern man, the greatest division is the one between Heaven and hell, between being *up* and feeling *down*. He desperately needs to take reality by the balls and re-connect with his lost arse! The effect is like having positive and negative charge coming together, Volt and Ampere and no resistance...This flicks a switch and there is—light!

"Positive" alone cannot do that, nor can light shine without darkness...

How would you know beauty, if you never look at shit? Where would you meditate anyway, if not in the shit-house?

Is shitting not the only direct act available to us humans, of *giving back to the earth* before we rot? We can do this reluctantly and squeamishly or we can celebrate it as a sacred act! We have that choice. Fight it or roll with it...

Don't hesitate to *enjoy* shitting! Try not to "do" it—instead meditate it!

The master never squeezes out the unripe banana!

It is the banana that squeezes itself through the blessed man...

It sensually massages itself past a grateful prostate, then opens up to the Mother Earth, and there it comes—a perfect manifestation of gratitude—a real, if modest gift to the Earth!

Woman might be reminded of birthing, and meditate accordingly to honour the Great Mother...

The most intimate gifts of the human body belong to the Earth, should be covered with earth and honored as Earth. Watch dog! He knows...

When the egg is laid, and it looks good as gold, smells fine, and you feel just great about your whole self—this will likely mean you are becoming conscious of your shit and are gradually getting ready to drop the bull.

You discover then that knowing your shit has made you a lot more honest with yourself!

You feel increasingly connected to truth, to your actual inner reality, and to energy.

Your first chakra is coming to life! You know harmony.

Only now are you getting ready to grow those great trees in your life, to scale your personal mountain, and to safely fly to all those holy places you read about in sacred scriptures and in nice-smelling books.

Other books by Fritz Blackburn:

- Travel-parenting

   - Chess-parenting

   - The Cosmic Egg
   - The Brink of Becoming
   - Tuko's Cave
   - Goddess Unleashed

About the Author

Fritz Blackburn studied law and economics at University Augsburg before traveling fulltime to remote cultures and learning shamanism and holistic healing. He lives in the bush in NZ with his wife Ikay, grows trees and writes culture-critical books.

www.ingramcontent.com/pod-product-compliance
Lightning Source LLC
Chambersburg PA
CBHW051455130726
47987CB00005B/2324